Geoff Dyer was born in Cheltenham in 1958. He is the author of *Ways of Telling*, a critical study of John Berger; the novels, *The Colour of Memory* and *The Search* (Penguin 1994); and *But Beautiful: A Book About Jazz*, which won the 1992 Somerset Maugham Prize and was shortlisted for the *Mail on Sunday*/John Llewellyn Rhys Memorial Prize.

Geoff Dyer's essays and reviews have appeared in the *Independent*, *New Writing*, *New Statesman & Society* and other periodicals. He writes regularly for the *Guardian* and is a contributing editor of *Esquire* magazine.

THE MISSING
OF THE SOMME

Geoff Dyer

PENGUIN BOOKS

PENGUIN BOOKS

Published by the Penguin Group
Penguin Books Ltd, 27 Wrights Lane, London W8 5TZ, England
Penguin Books USA Inc., 375 Hudson Street, New York, New York 10014, USA
Penguin Books Australia Ltd, Ringwood, Victoria, Australia
Penguin Books Canada Ltd, 10 Alcorn Avenue, Toronto, Ontario, Canada M4V 3B2
Penguin Books (NZ) Ltd, 182–190 Wairau Road, Auckland 10, New Zealand

Penguin Books Ltd, Registered Offices: Harmondsworth, Middlesex, England

First published by Hamish Hamilton 1994
Published in Penguin Books 1995
1 3 5 7 9 10 8 6 4 2

Excerpt from 'Grass' in Cornhuskers by Carl Sandburg, copyright 1918 by Holt, Rinehart and
Winston, Inc., and renewed 1946 by Carl Sandburg, reprinted by permission of Harcourt Brace &
Company. Lines from 'The Waste Land' in Collected Poems 1909–1962 by T. S. Eliot, reprinted by
kind permission of Faber & Faber.

Printed in England by Clays Ltd, St Ives plc

For my mother and father

'Remember: the past won't fit
into memory without something left over;
it must have a future.'

Joseph Brodsky

'A kaleidoscope of hypothetical contingencies . . .'

T. H. Thomas, reviewing Basil Liddell Hart's
The Real War *in 1931*

LIST OF ILLUSTRATIONS

ACKNOWLEDGEMENTS

I would like to thank my friends Paul Bonaventura, Chris Mitchell and Mark Hayhurst for reading an early draft of the manuscript and making many useful suggestions. (I am especially indebted to Mark whose quick reactions prevented us from getting killed – thanks to Paul's reckless driving – in Flanders.)

I am grateful to the editors of *Esquire*, the *Independent*, the *Observer* and *New Statesman & Society* for giving me space to try out draft versions of some of these pages; also to Patrick Early for the opportunity to lecture (in Belgrade of all places) on Wilfred Owen – and to David Punter for his helpful response to that lecture.

Thanks also to Iain Watson in Paris for encouragement and provocative suggestions, to Jeremy Young for his photographs, to Jane Pugh for the loan of an album of pictures, and to Xandra Hardie, Charles Drazin and Alexandra Pringle.

An award from the Kay Blundell Trust enabled me to complete the manuscript.

My ongoing debt to John Berger is too extensive to be adequately acknowledged here.

NOTE

Some quotations are not attributed in the text; full sources for all citations can be found in the notes. Throughout, Remembrance with an upper case 'R' refers to 'official' procedures such as the annual service at the Cenotaph; remembrance with a lower case 'r' to the more general and varied ways by which the war is remembered.

When I was a boy my grandfather took me to the Museum of Natural History. We saw animals, reptiles and sharks but, today, what I remember most clearly are the long uneven lines of butterflies framed in glass cases. On small cards the names of every specimen on display had been scrupulously recorded.

Row after row, bright and neat as medal ribbons.

'On every mantelpiece stand photographs wreathed with ivy,
smiling, true to the past . . .'

Dusty, bulging, old: they are all the same, these albums. The same faces, the same photos. Every family was touched by the war and every family has an album like this. Even as we prepare to open it, the act of looking at the album is overlaid by the emotions it will engender. We look at the pictures as if reading a poem about the experience of seeing them.

I turn the dark, heavy pages. The dust smell of old photographs.

The dead queuing up to enlist. Marching through the dark town, disappearing beyond the edge of the frame. Some turn up later, in the photos from hospital: marching away and convalescing, nothing in between. Always close to hand, the countryside seems empty in these later pictures, a register of absence. Dry stone walls and rivers. Portraits and group portraits. Officers and other ranks. The loved and the unloved, indistinguishable from each other.

'Memory has a spottiness,' writes Updike, 'as if the film was sprinkled with developer instead of immersed in it.' Each of these photos is marred, spotted, blotched; their imperfections make them seem like photos of memories. In some there is an encroaching white light, creeping over the image, wiping it out. Others are fading: photos of forgetting. Eventually nothing will remain but blank spaces.

A nurse in round glasses and long uniform ('Myself' printed beneath in my grandmother's perfect hand). A group of men in hospital. Two with patches over their eyes, three with arms in slings. One

> in his ghastly suit of grey,
> Legless, sewn short at the elbow.

2

A stern-faced sister stands at the end of the back row, each name diligently inked beneath the picture. My mother's father is the second on the left, in the back row.

Born (illegitimate) in Worthen in Shropshire, eighteen miles from Oswestry where Wilfred Owen was born. Farm labourer. Able only to read and write his name. Enlisted in 1914. Served on the Somme as a driver (of horses), where, according to family legend, he once went up to the front-line trenches in place of a friend whose courage had suddenly deserted him. Later, back in the reserve trench, he shovelled the remains of his best friend into a sandbag. (Every family has the same album, every family has a version of the same legend.) Returned to Shropshire in 1919 and resumed the life he had left.

Worked, went to war, married, worked.

He died aged ninety-one, able still only to write his name.

Everything I have said about my grandfather is true. Except he is not the man second from the left in the photograph. I do not know who that is. It makes no difference. He could be anyone's grandfather.

Like many young men, my grandfather was under age when he turned up to enlist. The recruiting sergeant told him to come back in a couple of days when he was two years older. My grandfather duly returned, added a couple of years to his age and was accepted into the army.

Similar episodes are fairly common in the repertoire of recruitment anecdotes, but I never doubted the veracity of this particular version of it, which my mother told several times over the years. It came as a surprise, then, to discover from his death certificate that my grandfather was born in November 1893 (the same year as Owen), and so was twenty when war broke out. One of the commonly circulating stories of the 1914 generation had been so thoroughly absorbed by my family that it had become part of my grandfather's biography.

He is everyone's grandfather.

★

Seven-thirty a.m. Mist lies over the fields of the Somme. Trees are smudged shapes. Nothing moves. Power lines sag and vanish over absent hedges. Birds call invisibly. Only the road can be sure of where it is going.

I stop for breakfast – an apple, a banana, yoghurt slurped from the carton – and consult the map I bought yesterday. A friend who was driving from Paris to catch a dawn ferry at Calais had given me a lift to Amiens. From there I hitched in the direction of Albert because, from my newly acquired map, it was the nearest station to the villages whose names I vaguely recognize: Beaumont-Hamel, Mametz, Pozières ... I want to visit the cemeteries on the Somme but have no clear idea of what they are like or which ones are particularly worth visiting. On my map, near Thiepval, is printed in heavy type: 'Memorial Brit.' When I began hitching this morning, I did not know what I would find or where I would go – I still don't, except that at some point in the day I will visit Thiepval. For now I cram everything back in my rucksack and continue walking.

Within an hour, exactly as forecast, the mist starts to thin. Level slopes of fields appear. The dusty blaze of rape. Dipping flatness. I walk towards a large cemetery, the most distant rows of headstones barely visible.

The cemetery is separated from the surrounding field by a low wall, dissolved in places by the linger of mist. Close to this wall a large cross appears as a mossy blur, like the trunk of a tree. The noise of the gate being unlatched sends birds flocking from branches and back. The gravel is loud beneath my feet. Near the gate, on a large stone – pale, horizontal, altar-like – is written:

THEIR NAME LIVETH FOR EVERMORE

Between this stone and the cross are rows of white headstones, bordered by perfect grass. Flowers: purple, dull red, flame-yellow.

Most of the headstones give simply the regiment, name, rank

and, where it is known, the date of the soldier's death, sometimes his age. Occasionally quotations have been added, but the elaborate biblical sentiments are superfluous; they neither add to nor detract from the uniform pathos of the headstones, some of which do not even bear a name:

A SOLDIER
OF THE GREAT WAR
KNOWN UNTO GOD

The cross has a bronze sword running down the centre, pointing to the ground. Gradually the mist thins enough for the cross to cast a promise of shadow, a darker haze, so faint it is barely there. Pale sunlight.

The high left-hand wall of the cemetery is a memorial to the New Zealand dead with no known graves 'who fell in the Battles of the Somme September and October 1916'. Inscribed along its length are 1,205 names.

Near the gate is a visitors' book and register of graves. The name of the cemetery is Caterpillar Valley. There are 5,539 men buried here.

'We will remember them'

The Great War ruptured the historical continuum, destroying the legacy of the past. Wyndham Lewis sounds the characteristic note when he calls it 'the turning-point in the history of the earth', but there is a sense in which, for the British at least, the war helped to preserve the past even as it destroyed it. Life in the decade and a half preceding 1914 has come to be viewed inevitably and unavoidably through the optic of the war that followed it. The past *as past* was preserved by the war that shattered it. By ushering in a future characterized by instability and uncertainty, it embalmed for ever a past characterized by stability and certainty.

Things were, of course, less settled than the habitual view of pre-August 1914 tempts us to believe. For many contemporary observers the war tainted the past, revealing and making explicit a violence that had been latent in the preceding peace. Eighty years on, this sense of crouched and gathering violence has been all but totally filtered out of our perception of the pre-war period. Militant suffragettes, class unrest, strikes, Ireland teetering on the brink of civil war – all are shaded and softened by the long, elegiac shadows cast by the war.

European civilization may have been 'breaking down even before war destroyed it', but our abiding sense of the quietness of the Edwardian frame of mind is, overwhelmingly, derived from and enhanced by the holocaust that followed it. The glorious summer of 1914 seems, even, to have been generated by the cataclysm that succeeded it.

In a persuasive passage, Johan Huizinga admonished the historian to

maintain towards his subject an indeterminist point of view. He must constantly put himself at a point in the past at which the known factors still seem to permit different outcomes.

But history does not lie uniformly over events. Here and there it forms drifts – and these drifts are at their deepest between the years 1914 and 1918. Watching footage of the Normandy landings, we can experience D-Day *as it happened*. History hangs in the balance, waiting to be made. The Battle of the Somme, by contrast, is deeply buried in its own aftermath. The euphoric intoxication of the early days of the French Revolution – 'Bliss was it in that dawn' – remains undiminished by the terror lying in wait a few chapters on. The young men queuing up to enlist in 1914 have the look of ghosts. They are queuing up to be slaughtered: they are already dead. By Huizinga's terms, the Great War urges us to write the opposite of history: the story of effects generating their cause.

They shall grow not old, as we that are left grow old:
Age shall not weary them, nor the years condemn.
At the going down of the sun and in the morning
We will remember them.

These incantatory rhythms and mantra-like repetitions are intoned every year on Remembrance Day. They are words we hear but rarely see in print. We know them – more or less – by heart. They seem not to have been written but to have pulsed into life in the nation's collective memory, to have been generated, down the long passage of years, by the hypnotic spell of Remembrance they are used to induce.

But they *were* written, of course, by Laurence Binyon, in September 1914: *before* the fallen actually fell. 'For the Fallen', in other words, is a work not of remembrance but of anticipation, or more accurately, the *anticipation of remembrance*: a foreseeing that is also a determining.

On 22 August 1917 at Pilkem Ridge near Ypres, Ernest Brooks took one of the iconographic photographs of the Great War. Head bowed, rifle on his back, a soldier is silhouetted against the going down of the sun, looking at the grave of a dead comrade, remembering him. A photograph from the war – the Battle of Third Ypres (or Passchendaele as it is better known) was still raging, the armistice was fifteen months distant – it is also a photograph of the way the war will come to be remembered. It is a photograph of the future, of the future's view of the past. It is a photograph of Binyon's poem, of a sentiment. We *will* remember them.

If several of the terms by which we remember the war were established in advance of its conclusion, many crucial elements were embodied in a single dramatic event two years before it started.

Between November 1911 and January 1912 two teams of men – one British, headed by a naval officer, Robert Falcon

7

The anticipation of memory

Scott, the other Norwegian, headed by Roald Amundsen – were engaged in the last stage of a protracted race to the South Pole. Using dogs and adapting themselves skilfully to the hostile environment, the Norwegian team reached the Pole on 15 December and returned safely. Scott, leader of an ill-prepared expedition which relied on strength-sapping man-hauling, reached the Pole on 17 January. Defeated, the five-man team faced a gruelling 800-mile trudge back to safety. By 21 March, eleven miles from the nearest depot of food and fuel, the three exhausted surviving members of the expedition – Scott, Dr Edward Wilson and Henry Bowers – pitched their tent and sat out a blizzard. At some point Scott seems to have made the decision that it was better to stay put and preserve the record of their struggle rather than die in their tracks. They survived for at least nine days while Scott, in Roland Huntford's phrase, 'prepared his exit from the stage' and addressed letters to posterity: 'We are setting a good example to our countrymen, if not by getting into a tight place, by facing it like men when we get there.' Despite its failure, the expedition, wrote Scott, 'has shown that Englishmen can endure hardships, help one another and meet death with as great a fortitude as ever in the past'. The tradition of heroic death which aggrandizes his own example is also invigorated by it: 'We are showing that Englishmen can still die with a bold spirit, fighting it out to the end . . . I think this makes an example for Englishmen of the future.'

On 12 November, in the collapsed tent, the bodies and their documents were found by a rescue party and the legend of Scott of the Antarctic began to take immediate effect. 'Of their suffering, hardship and devotion to one another,' wrote a member of the rescue team, 'the world will soon know the deeds that were done were equally as great as any committed on Battlefield and won the respect and honour of every true Britisher.'

Scott's headstrong incompetence had actually meant that, from an early stage, the expedition had been riddled by tension. Captain Oates – the 'very gallant Englishman' of legend – had earlier written that 'if Scott fails to get to the Pole he jolly well deserves it'. Although clad in the guise of scientific discovery, Scott's expedition contributed nothing to the knowledge of polar travel unless it was to emphasize 'the grotesque futility of man-hauling'. But with Scott, futility (the title of one of only a handful of poems published by Wilfred Owen in his lifetime) becomes an important component of the heroic. That Scott had turned the expedition into an affair of 'heroism for heroism's sake' only enhanced the posthumous glory that greeted news of his death when it reached England on 11 February the following year.

A memorial service 'for one of the most inefficient of polar expeditions, and one of the worst of polar explorers' was held at St Paul's, and Scott's failure took its place alongside Nelson's victory at Trafalgar as a triumphant expression of the British spirit. Scott's distorting, highly rhetorical version of events was taken up enthusiastically and unquestioningly by the nation as a whole. At the naval dockyard chapel in Devonport, the sermon emphasized 'the glory of self-sacrifice, the blessing of failure'. By now the glorious failure personified by Scott had become a British ideal: a vivid example of how 'to make a virtue of calamity and dress up incompetence as heroism'.

That the story of Scott anticipates the larger heroic calamity of the Great War hardly needs emphasizing. As a now-forgotten writer put it, he had given his

countrymen an example of endurance ... We have so many heroes among us now, so many Scotts ... holding sacrifice above gain [and] we begin to understand what a splendour arises from the bloody fields ... of Flanders.

In Huntingdon, on Armistice Day 1923, a war memorial was unveiled. The statue is of a soldier resting, one foot propped on the wall behind him. The protruding knee supports his left arm which in turn supports his chin in a quizzical echo of Rodin's *Thinker*. His other hand steadies the rifle and bayonet propped beside him. The figure was sculpted by Kathleen Scott, widow of Scott of the Antarctic.

Discussion about the form memorials like this should take was widespread and well advanced before the war ended. By 1917 associations and clubs across the country were meeting to establish appropriate means of remembrance.* By the early twenties

* As early as 1915 the Church Crafts League was making 'a special effort to direct the pious intentions of bereaved relatives into the proper channels'. On 8 January 1916 the Civic Arts Association held a conference on how best to ensure that the dead were suitably remembered. Six months later the same association organized 'An Exhibition of Designs for War Memorials'. In the same year the Royal Academy set up a committee of influential architects and sculptors to offer guidance on the aesthetics of remembrance. The following June various public bodies met at the Royal Academy 'to secure combined instead of isolated efforts in erecting memorials and to protect churches and public buildings from unsuitable treatment in setting up monuments of the war'.

the nation's grief had been sculpted into a broadly agreed form. Although permitting of many variations, this was the form sketched in September 1916 when the *Cornhill Magazine* argued against allegory in favour of 'simplicity of statement ... so that the gazer can see at once that the matter recorded is great and significant, and desires to know more'.

At the end of the war a counter-case was still being made for memorials which would have practical rather than simply poetic value: hospitals, homes, universities. Such proposals were more in keeping with the mood of 1945 than 1918 when the *need* was for a memorial idiom and architecture unencumbered by questions of utility. In 1945 that architecture and idiom were in place: all that was needed was to add new names and dates. The real task was to rebuild an economy and infrastructure shattered by war.

Whatever the human cost, the Second World War had an obvious practical purpose and goal – one that became especially clear retrospectively after footage of Hitler's death camps became public. After the Great War people had little clear idea of why it had been fought or what had been accomplished except for the loss of millions of lives. This actually made the task of memorializing the war relatively easy.

Memorials to the Second World War and the Holocaust are still being constructed all over the world; the form they should take is still being debated. Controversy – over the 'Bomber' Harris statue in London, for example – punctuates each phase of the Second World War as it is replayed along the length of its fiftieth anniversary. The form of memorials to the Great War, by contrast, was agreed on and fixed definitively and relatively quickly. By the mid-thirties the public construction of memory was complete. Since then only a few memorials have been built: addenda to the text of memory. All that needed to be added was time: time for the past to seep into future memory and take root there.

The exact number of people who died in the Great War will never be known. France and Germany each lost more than a million and a half men; Russia, two million. Three-quarters of a million of the dead were British – a figure which rises to almost a million when the losses of the Empire as a whole are considered.

During the war the dead were buried haphazardly, often in mass graves. By the time of the great battles of attrition of 1916–17 mass graves were dug in advance of major offensives. Singing columns of soldiers fell grimly silent as they marched by these gaping pits en route to the front-line trenches. Those who died in the midst of fiercely protracted fighting could lie and rot for months or years before being buried. Others would be buried in isolated individual graves or small, improvised cemeteries. Sir Edwin Lutyens, one of the architects responsible for the cemeteries we see today, visited France in 1917 and was moved by the hurriedly constructed wartime graves. On 12 July he jotted down his impressions in a letter to his wife:

The graveyards, haphazard from the needs of much to do and little time for thought. And then a ribbon of isolated graves like a milky way across miles of country where men were tucked in where they fell. Ribbons of little crosses each touching each across a cemetery, set in a wilderness of annuals and where one sort of flower is grown the effect is charming, easy and oh so pathetic. One thinks for the moment no other monument is needed.

Such feelings, as Lutyens himself realized, were transitory; for the future more enduring monuments were needed. Accordingly, after the armistice, under the auspices of the Imperial War Graves Commission, work began on establishing the cemeteries as permanent memorials to the dead.*

Despite protests, culminating in a debate at the House of

* Until 1917 the Imperial War Graves Commission was known as the Graves Registration Commission; in 1960 it became the Commonwealth War Graves Commission.

'One thinks for the moment no other monument is needed'
– Lutyens

Commons on 4 May 1920 in which the proposals were condemned as 'hideous and unchristian', it was decided that there
would be no repatriation or private memorials. All British and
Empire soldiers would be buried – or would remain buried –
where they fell. Undifferentiated by rank, uniform headstones –
cheaper to produce and easier to preserve than crosses, compatible with a range of religious (dis)belief – would achieve an
'equality in death'; the name of every soldier who died would
be recorded, either in a cemetery or – where no body was
found – on one of a number of memorials. At the base of each
headstone there would be space for the next of kin to add
inscriptions of their own.

Such an undertaking was without precedent but not without
a prehistory. The war dead may not have merited cemeteries of
their own in earlier centuries, but in some ways the military
cemeteries of the Great War represent the culmination and
systematic application of developments in *civilian* cemetery
design. These developments were themselves emblematic of the
way attitudes towards death had been changing since the Enlight-
enment. As the spectre of plague receded, so, in George Mosse's

striking phrase, 'the image of the grim reaper was replaced by the image of death as eternal sleep'. A growing awareness of the link between poor hygiene and illness – and a corresponding association between foul odours and death – saw cemeteries being built away from crowded towns in quiet, shaded settings, in environments conducive to rest. Setting and symbolism encouraged a mood of pantheistic reflection rather than penitence and fear.

Three architects – Lutyens, Sir Herbert Baker and Sir Reginald Blomfield – were given overall responsibility for implementing the principles established by the Commission: white headstones undifferentiated by rank, the Great War Stone with the inscription 'Their name liveth for evermore' (chosen by Rudyard Kipling) from *Ecclesiasticus*. Lutyens wanted the cemeteries to be non-denominational, but was forced to accept the inclusion of Blomfield's Cross of Sacrifice: the sword of war sheathed by the cross, a simple reconciliation of the martial and the Christian.

With so many graves scattered over the battlefields, bodies had sometimes to be exhumed from the smaller cemeteries and re-interred in larger, or 'concentration', plots – though frequently these 'new' sites were themselves extensions of original battlefield cemeteries. Some were named after regiments or battalions, but, wherever possible, the wartime names were retained: Railway Hollow, Blighty Valley, Crucifix Corner, Owl Trench...

Even after this process of rationalization hundreds of British and Commonwealth cemeteries were spread over Flanders and northern France. The first were completed by 1920, but work continued throughout the decade. By 1934, in the *département* of the Somme alone, 150,000 British and Commonwealth dead had been buried in 242 cemeteries. In total 918 cemeteries were built on the Western Front with 580,000 named and 180,000 unidentified graves. A few cemeteries were kept – and remain – 'open' to bury bodies discovered after the official searches had been completed, in September 1921. Between then and the outbreak of the Second World War, in spite of the major battlefields having been searched as many as six times, the remains of 38,000 men were discovered in Belgium and France. The bodies of the missing still continue to reappear: pushed to the surface by the slow tidal movement of the soil, unearthed by farmers ploughing their fields.

The design is always broadly similar, but each cemetery – due to its location, size, layout and the selection of flowers – has its own distinctive character and feel. Some, like the Serre Road cemeteries, are, in Kipling's phrase, vast 'silent cities'. Others are very small, tucked away in a corner of a field, in the crook of a stream, at the shaded edge of a wood.

All, whether large or small, are scrupulously maintained, immaculate. This is strange: cemeteries, after all, are expected to age. In these military cemeteries there is no ageing: everything is kept as new. Time does not exist here, only the seasons. The cemeteries look now exactly as they did sixty years ago.

Then as now the official idiom of Remembrance stressed not so much victory or patriotic triumph as Sacrifice. Sacrifice may have been a euphemism for slaughter but, either way, the significance of victory was overwhelmed by the human cost of achieving it. As if acknowledging that, in this respect, there was little to choose between victory and defeat, between the British and German experience of the war, memorial inscriptions were not to 'Our' but to '*The* Glorious Dead'.

The war, it begins to seem, had been fought in order that it might be remembered, that it might live up to its memory.

Even while it was raging, the characteristic attitude of the war was *to look forward to the time when it would be remembered*. ' "The future!" ' exclaims Bertrand, one of the soldiers in Henri Barbusse's *Under Fire*.

'How will they regard this slaughter, they who'll live after us ... How will they regard these exploits which even we who perform them don't know whether one should compare them with those of Plutarch's and Corneille's heroes or with those of hooligans and apaches.'*

He stood up with his arms still crossed. His face, as profoundly serious as a statue's, drooped upon his chest. But he emerged once again from his marble muteness to repeat, 'The future, the future! The work of the future will be to wipe out the present, to wipe it out more than we can imagine, to wipe it out like something abominable and shameful. And yet – this present – it had to be, it had to be!'

Published in France as *Le Feu* in 1916 and translated into English the following year, Barbusse's novel was the first major work of prose to give fictional expression to the experience of the war. A direct influence on Owen and Siegfried Sassoon, it established an imaginative paradigm for much subsequent writing about the war. The passage quoted is crucial, not simply for the content of Bertrand's speech but for the manner in which Barbusse presents it. The sculptural similes are especially telling. With his 'marble muteness' and face like a statue Bertrand becomes, literally, a monument to this present which will, he alleges, be wiped out.

In the final chapter of the book there is a related, equally revealing passage. Following a terrible bombardment the soldiers wake to a nightmare dawn and fall to talking about the impossibility of conveying what went on during the war to anyone who was not there.

'It'll be no good telling about it, eh? They wouldn't believe you; not out of malice or through liking to pull your leg, but because they couldn't ... No one can know it. Only us.'

'No, not even us, not even us!' someone cried.

* Bertrand's words are echoed by those of an actual French soldier, Sergeant Marc Boassoan, who wrote to his wife in a letter of July 1916: 'What kind of a nation will they make of us tomorrow, these exhausted creatures, emptied of blood, emptied of thought, crushed by superhuman fatigue?'

'That's what I say too. We shall forget – we're forgetting already, my boy!'

'We've seen too much to remember.'

'And everything we've seen was too much. We're not *made* to hold it all. It takes its bloody hook in all directions. We're too little to hold it.'

The person whose opinions begin this passage speaks 'sorrowfully, like a bell'. Anticipating Owen – 'What passing-bells for these who die as cattle?' – the discussion turns to whether there can be any adequate recognition of those who have suffered so much. Barbusse also anticipates Owen in his response: by itemizing everything that will be forgotten. 'We will remember them,' intones Binyon. ' "We *shall* forget!" ' exclaims one of Barbusse's soldiers,

'Not only the length of the big misery, which can't be reckoned, as you say, ever since the beginning, but the marches that turn up the ground and turn it up again, lacerating your feet and wearing out your bones under a load that seems to grow bigger in the sky, the exhaustion until you don't know your own name any more, the tramping and the inaction that grinds you, the digging jobs that exceed your strength, the endless vigils when you fight against sleep and watch for an enemy who is everywhere in the night, the pillows of dung and lice – we shall forget not only those, but even the foul wounds of the shells and machine-guns, the mines, the gas, and the counter-attacks. At those moments you're full of the excitement of reality, and you've some satisfaction. But all that wears off and goes away, you don't know how and you don't know where, and there's only the names left...'

Sassoon's later claim – 'Remembering, we forget' – is inverted: a memorial is constructed from the litany of what will be forgotten. At the end of it all, as with a memorial, there are 'only the names left'.

'We're forgetting-machines,' exclaims another of Barbusse's soldiers. Accompanying the draft preface Owen wrote for a proposed collection of his poems was a list of possible contents;

next to the first poem, 'Miners', is scribbled 'How the future will forget'. Constantly reiterated, the claim that we are in danger of forgetting is one of the ways in which the war ensured it would be remembered. Every generation since the armistice has believed that it will be the last for whom the Great War has any meaning. Now, when the last survivors are within a few years of their deaths, I too wonder if the memory of the war will perish with the generation after mine. This sense of imminent amnesia is, has been and – presumably – always will be immanent in the war's enduring memory.

The issue, in short, is not simply the way the war generates memory but the way memory has determined – and continues to determine – the meaning of the war.

Taken from his earlier poem 'Recessional', Kipling's words 'Lest we Forget' admonish us from memorials all over the country. Forget what? And what will befall us if we *do* forget? It takes a perverse effort of will to ask such questions – for, translated into words, the dates 1914–18 have come to mean 'that which is incapable of being forgotten'.

Sassoon expended a good deal of satirical bile on the hypocrisy of official modes of Remembrance but no one was more troubled by the reciprocity of remembering and forgetting. He may claim, in 'Dreamers', that soldiers draw 'no dividends from time's tomorrows', but he is determined that they will have a place in all our yesterdays.

As early as March 1919, the poem 'Aftermath' opens with the aghast question, '*Have you forgotten yet? . . .*' Sassoon's tone is no less admonitory than Kipling's – '*Look down, and swear by the slain of the War that you'll never forget*' – but in place of august memorials he wants to cram our nostrils with the smell of the trenches:

Do you remember the rats; and the stench
Of corpses rotting in front of the front-line trench –
And dawn coming, dirty-white, and chill with a hopeless rain?

Beating his familiar drum, Sassoon, in his 1933 sequence 'The Road to Ruin', imagined 'the Prince of Darkness' standing in front of the Cenotaph, intoning:

> Make them forget, O Lord, what this Memorial
> Means . . .

Over the years, passing by in a bus or on a bike, I have seen the Cenotaph so often that I scarcely notice it. It has become part of the unheeded architecture of the everyday. The empty tomb has become the invisible tomb.

In the years following the armistice, however, especially in 1919 and 1920, the Cenotaph, in Stephen Graham's words, 'gather[ed] to itself all the experience and all that was sacred in the war'.

A victory parade had been planned for 19 July 1919, but the Prime Minister, Lloyd George, opposed any proposals for national rejoicing which did not include 'some tribute to the dead'. Lutyens was duly asked to devise a temporary, non-denominational 'catafalque'. In a matter of hours he sketched the design for what became the Cenotaph.

The wood and plaster pylon was unveiled on schedule, but such was the emotion aroused by its stern, ascetic majesty that it was decided – 'by the human sentiment of millions', as Lutyens himself wrote – to replace it with an identical permanent version made of Portland stone.

In the meantime the temporary structure remained in place for the first anniversary of Armistice Day when the two minutes' silence was first introduced.

Since the Second World War, when it was decided to commemorate the memory of the dead of both wars on the Sunday closest to the eleventh of November, the effect of the silence has been muted. On the normally busy weekdays between the wars –

especially in 1919 and 1920 – the effect of 'the great awful silence' was overwhelming, shattering.

In 1919, at eleven a.m., not only in Britain but throughout the Empire, all activity ceased. Traffic came to a standstill. In workshops and factories and at the Stock Exchange no one moved. In London not a single telephone call was made. Trains scheduled to leave at eleven delayed their departures by two minutes; those already in motion stopped. In Nottingham Assize Court a demobbed soldier was being tried for murder. At eleven o'clock the whole court, including the prisoner, stood silently for two minutes. Later in the day the soldier was sentenced to death.

On 12 November 1919 the *Manchester Guardian* reported the previous day's silence:

The first stroke of eleven produced a magical effect. The tram cars glided into stillness, motors ceased to cough and fume and stopped dead, and the mighty-limbed dray-horses hunched back upon their loads and stopped also, seeming to do it of their own volition ... Someone took off his hat, and with a nervous hesitancy the rest of the men bowed their heads also. Here and there an old soldier could be detected slipping unconsciously into the posture of 'attention'. An elderly woman, not far away, wiped her eyes and the man beside her looked white and stern. Everyone stood very still ... The hush deepened. It had spread over the whole city and become so pronounced as to impress one with a sense of audibility. It was ... a silence which was almost pain ... And the spirit of memory brooded over it all.

The following year the silence and the unveiling of the permanent Cenotaph were complemented by another even more emotive component of the ceremony of Remembrance: the burial of the Unknown Warrior.

Eight unmarked graves were exhumed from the most important battlefields of the war. Blindfolded, a senior officer selected one coffin at random.* In an elaborate series of symbol-packed rituals 'the man who had been nothing and who was now to be everything' was carried through France with full battle honours and transported across the Channel in the destroyer *Verdun* (so that this battle and the soldiers of France also found a place in the proceedings). On the morning of the 11th the flag-draped coffin was taken by gun carriage to Whitehall, where, at eleven o'clock, the permanent Cenotaph was unveiled.

The weather played its part. The sun shone through a haze of cloud. There was no wind. Flags, at half mast, hung in folds. No wind disturbed the silence which descended once again. Big Ben struck eleven. The last stroke dissolved over London, spreading a silence through the nation. 'In silence, broken only by a nearby sob,' reported *The Times*, 'the great multitude bowed its head . . .' People held their breath lest they should be heard in the stillness. The quiet, which had seemed already to have reached its limit, grew deeper and even deeper. A woman's shriek

---

* The anaesthetized solemnity of this process of selection is savagely undermined by John Dos Passos in *Nineteen Nineteen*, the second volume of his *USA* trilogy:

> In the tarpaper morgue at Châlons-sur-Marne in the reek of chloride of lime and the dead, they picked out the pine box that held all that was left of
> enie menie minie moe plenty other pine boxes stacked up there containing what they'd scraped up of Richard Roe
> and other person or persons unknown. Only one can go. How did they pick John Doe?
> Make sure he ain't a dinge, boys.
> make sure he ain't a guinea or a kike,
> how can you tell a guy's a hundredpercent when all you've got's a gunnysack full of bones, bronze buttons stamped with the screaming eagle and a pair of roll puttees?
> . . . and the gagging chloride and the puky dirtstench of the yearold dead . . .

A similarly ironic palaver surrounds the choosing of the French Unknown Soldier in Bertrand Tavernier's 1989 film *La Vie et rien d'autre* (*Life and Nothing But*).

'rose and fell and rose again' until the silence 'bore down once more'.

O God, our help in ages past.

The silence stretched on until, 'suddenly, acute, shattering, the very voice of pain itself – but pain triumphant – rose the clear notes of the bugles in The Last Post'.

From the Cenotaph the carriage bearing the Unknown Warrior made its way to Westminster Abbey. Inside, the same intensity of emotion was reinforced by numerical arrangement: a thousand bereaved widows and mothers; a hundred nurses wounded or blinded in the war; a guard of honour made up of a hundred men who had won the Victoria Cross, fifty on each side of the nave. The highest-ranking commanders from the war were among the pallbearers: Haig, French and Trenchard. The king scattered earth from the soil of France on to the coffin. 'All this,' commented one observer, 'was to stir such memories and emotions as might have made the very stones cry out.'

A photograph of the temporary Cenotaph of 1919: soldiers marching past, huge crowds looking on. There is nothing triumphant about the parade. The role of the army is not to celebrate victory but to represent the dead. This is an inevitable side-effect of the language of Remembrance being permeated so thoroughly by the idea of sacrifice. In honouring the dead, survivors testified to their exclusion from the war's ultimate meaning – sacrifice – except vicariously as witnesses. The role of the living is to offer tribute, not to receive it. The soldiers marching past the Cenotaph, in other words, comprise an army of the surrogate dead.

In an effort to give some sense of the scale of the loss, Fabian Ware, head of the Imperial War Graves Commission, pointed out that if the Empire's dead marched four abreast down Whitehall, it

The surrogate dead

would take them three and a half days to pass the Cenotaph.★
Over a million of the living passed by between its unveiling on
11 November and the sealing of the Unknown Warrior's tomb

★ Bertrand Tavernier's *Life and Nothing But* ends with Major Dellaplane's
(Philippe Noiret) calculation that it would take the French dead eleven days
and nights to march up the Champs-Elysées to the Arc de Triomphe.

23

a week later. The correspondence between Ware's image and what actually took place in 1920 is such that to anyone looking at this photo the soldiers seem like the dead themselves, marching back to receive the tribute of the living. Ware's hypothetical idea was made flesh. 'The dead lived again,' wrote a reporter in *The Times*.

'A crowd flowed over Westminster Bridge. So many, / I had not thought death had undone so many,' wrote T. S. Eliot in *The Waste Land*.

The line of soldiers marching past the Cenotaph stretches out of sight, out of time. If we followed the line, it would take us back to another photograph, of men marching away to war. These two images are really simply two segments of a single picture of the long march through the war. There is a single column of men, so long that by the time those at the back are marching off from the recruiting stations, heading to trains, those at the front – the dead – are marching past the Cenotaph.

An early draft of Wilfred Owen's 'Apologia Pro Poemate Meo' is entitled 'The Unsaid'. In an accidental echo of Owen, John Berger has written that the two minutes' silence

was a silence before the untellable. The sculptured war memorials are like no other public monuments ever constructed. They are numb: monuments to an inexpressible calamity.

The Cenotaph is the starkest embodiment of Berger's claim. It is a representation in three dimensions of the silence that surrounded it for two minutes on Armistice Day. The public wanted a permanent version of the Cenotaph to record – to hold – the silence that was gathered within it and which, thereafter, would emanate from it. During the silence it had seemed, according to *The Times*, as if 'the very pulse of Time stood still'. In recording that silence, the Cenotaph would also be an emblem of timelessness. A temporary version of the Cenotaph was an impossible contradiction: it had to be permanent.

For two minutes in each of the years that followed, the silence of the monument was recharged. Since the Second World War and the diminished power of the Sunday Silence, that silence has drained from the Cenotaph. The clamour of London encroaches on it annually; its silence is becoming inaudible, fading.

In the 1920s neither the permanent Cenotaph nor the Unknown Warrior could satisfy the passion for remembrance. In many ways the means of remembrance, like the war itself, were self-generating. In 1921 the British Legion instituted the sale of Flanders poppies – eight million of them – which has continued, in manufactured form, to the present day. Two years after its inauguration in 1927, the British Legion Festival of Remembrance introduced its most distinctive and moving feature whereby a million poppies, each one representing a life, flutter down on to the servicemen assembled below.

Monuments, meanwhile, were being unveiled throughout Britain; cemeteries were being built in France and Belgium; the names of the dead appeared on regimental memorials and rolls of honour in places of work and trade associations, cities and villages, universities and schools.*

While this made the human cost of the war more apparent, the scale of the loss, it turned out, could actually be comforting. The pain of mothers, wives and fathers was subsumed in a list of names whose sheer scale was numbing. In the course of the war the casualties had been played down. Then, realizing that grief could be rendered more manageable if simultaneously divided

* This scrupulous recording of the dead was due both to the unprecedented scale of loss and to the fact that those who died, whether volunteers or conscripts, were, for the most part, citizen-soldiers. The principle of honouring the war dead individually can be traced back to the French Revolution and the dawn of the citizen-army – but it was not until the Great War that the dead were comprehensively commemorated. Although there were exceptions, the common soldier before 1914 was, in George Mosse's words, 'treated as part of an anonymous collectivity'. The Great War was the first to give equal honour to all the dead, officers and men alike.

The construction of memory

and shared by a million, the scale of sacrifice was emphasized. Publicizing the scale of the loss was the best way to make it bearable.

And was there not, amidst all this grief, a faint shudder or shiver of excitement at the unimaginable vastness of it all? The war had set all kinds of records in terms of scale: the greatest bombardments ever seen, the biggest guns, shells and mines, the biggest mobilization, the greatest loss of life ('the million dead'). Was there not a faint glow of pride, an unavoidable undertow of semantic approval, in terming the war 'Great'?

Covered by a patina of sorrow though it may be, something of this quality perhaps endures to this day, perpetuated by writers who, myself included, prefer this appellation with all its elegiac resonance to that stark numerical designation, 'The First World War'.

'Horrible beastliness of war'

'Great' or 'First World', any book about the war, or commentary on the literature or art it produced, will stress its *horror*. The largest entry in the latent index of any such book will always be: 'War, horror of'. Before we have even settled down to read the first stanza of Owen's 'Dulce et Decorum Est', we are already murmuring to ourselves the old mantra, 'the horror of war'.

War may be horrible, but that should not distract us from acknowledging what a horrible cliché this has become. The coinage has been worn so thin that its value seems only marginally greater than 'Glory', 'Sacrifice' or 'Pro Patria', which 'horror' condemns as counterfeit. The phrase 'horror of war' has become so automatic a conjunction that it conveys none of the horror it is meant to express.

Partly this over-use is a product of decorum. One cannot, in good taste, dwell on death, mutilation and injury without stressing their horror. Horror, consequently, becomes a mere formality, a form of words. One is reminded, also, of washing-powder commercials, which have relied for so long on prefixing brand names with 'new improved' that the expression has actually come to mean 'same old'. The words have bleached themselves out, become an unnoticed part of the brand name. To convey the new and improved nature of the product you have to add a prefix to the prefix: New Improved New Improved Ariel.

'The horror of war' has become similarly self-erasing. A review from *The Times Educational Supplement*, quoted on the back of the paperback edition of Lyn Macdonald's *1914–1918: Voices and Images of the Great War*, stresses 'the sickening repetitive monotony of hopeless horror'. 'Horror' on its own, in other words, has no power to horrify. The more you pile it on like this, the faster linguistic wear proceeds. Having emphasized that the scenes in Paul Nash's paintings are not simply appalling but 'grimly appalling', Nigel Viney, in *Images of Wartime*, soon finds himself descending into 'the very depths of infinite horror'.

The most horrific aspect of the Great War was the waste of lives as men were sent to the front in battles of meaningless attrition. Is their cause served appropriately, one wonders, by a verbal strategy which relies, for its meaning, on constantly reinforcing attrition?

Strings of shuddering adjectives dull the reaction they are intended to induce. The calm, measured tread of Elaine Scarry's formulation, by contrast, is terrible in its simplicity: 'The main purpose and outcome of war is injuring.'

'Before the Great War there was no war poetry as we now conceive the term,' writes Peter Parker in *The Old Lie*; 'instead there was martial verse.' So pervasive were the conventions of feeling produced by this tradition that in 1914 the eleven-year-old Eric Blair could write a heartfelt poem – 'Awake, young men of England' – relying entirely on received sentiment. In exactly the same way, an eleven-year-old writing fifty years on could, in similar circumstances, come up with a heartfelt poem expressing the horror of war – while also relying solely on received sentiment.

In some ways, then, we talk of the horror of war as instinctively and enthusiastically as Rupert Brooke and his contemporaries jumped at the chance of war 'like swimmers into cleanness leaping'.

This is not just a linguistic quibble. Off-the-peg formulae free you from thinking for yourself about what is being said. Whenever words are bandied about automatically and easily, their meaning is in the process of leaking away or evaporating. The ease with which Rupert Brooke coined his 'think only this of me' heroics by embracing a ready-made formula of feeling should alert us to – and make us sceptical of – the ease with which these sentiments have been overruled by another. Isaac Rosenberg acutely condemned Rupert Brooke's 'begloried sonnets' for their reliance on 'second-hand phrases'. But there is a similarly second- or third-hand whiff to critic Keith Sagar's indignant characterization of Armistice Day as

part of the process whereby the nation promises to remember for one day a year in order to be able to forget with a clear conscience for the other three hundred and sixty-four; the process whereby the nation accepts with pride the slaughter of a whole generation of its youth. The rhetoric of the Cenotaph ceremony is a continuance in solemn guise of the lying jingoism which prompted Owen to write three months before his death: 'I wish the Boche would have the pluck to come right in and make a clean sweep of the pleasure boats, and the promenaders on the spa, and all the stinking Leeds and Bradford war-profiteers . . .'

Owen is regularly invoked to challenge or undermine the official procedures of Remembrance in this way, but our memory of the Great War actually depends on the mutual support of these two ostensibly opposed coordinates: the Unknown Soldier and the poet everyone knows.

Owen was born in Shropshire on 18 March 1893. He was teaching in France when war was declared but volunteered for the Artists' Rifles in 1915. Under the influence of Sassoon, whom he met at Craiglockhart Hospital in 1917 while suffering from shell-shock, he began writing the war poems on which his reputation rests. He returned to France and was killed in action a week before the armistice, aged twenty-five.

The extreme brevity of his life is brought out by Jon Stallworthy's *Wilfred Owen*, the standard biography. Since Stallworthy diligently allots more or less the same amount of space to each phase of Owen's life, by the time we come to the part we're most interested in, the period of his major poems, we realize with a shock that there is only a fraction of the book left. It is as if the remaining 700 pages of a standard-sized life have simply been ripped out. Not only that, but in his last weeks we lose sight of Owen as an individual (there are no eyewitness accounts of his death) and have to resort to the wide-angle of regimental history. Dominic Hibberd has fleshed out this period somewhat in *Wilfred Owen: The Last Year*, but both books stop where Owen's life really begins – with his death.

In his lifetime Owen published only five poems ('Song of Songs', 'The Next War', 'Miners', 'Hospital Barge' and 'Futility'). Seven appeared in Edith Sitwell's *Wheels* anthology of 1919; a slim selection, edited by Sassoon, came out the following year; Edmund Blunden's more substantial edition was published in 1931. This means that Owen's poems came to the notice of the public not as gestures of *protest* but as part of a larger structure of *bereavement*.

The period from the armistice onwards saw the construction of memorials throughout England and cemeteries throughout Flanders and northern France. Climaxing with a flash flood of war memoirs and novels in the late 1920s,* this phase of pro-

* inter alia: 1926: Herbert Read, *In Retreat*; 1928: Edmund Bunden, *Undertones of War*; Siegfried Sassoon, *Memoirs of a Fox-Hunting Man*; E. E. Cummings, *The Enormous Room*; Erich Maria Remarque, *All Quiet on the Western Front*;

tracted mourning was formally completed with the inauguration of the Memorial to the Missing of the Somme at Thiepval in 1932.

The extent to which the strands of this fabric of loss are intertwined can be glimpsed by the way that in 1931 Blunden borrowed the 'official' vocabulary of Remembrance to lament 'how great a *glory* had departed' from the world of poetry with Owen's death.

In the years following the armistice the anti-war spirit was so strong that, as the mature Eric Blair (George Orwell) noted, 'even the men who had been slaughtered were held in some way to blame'. But the hope that the anti-war case had been clinched for good, on the other hand – by the war poets particularly and by Owen especially – proved short-lived.

Christopher Isherwood, who was born in 1904, the year after Orwell, recalls that 'we young writers of the middle twenties were all suffering, more or less consciously, from a feeling of shame that we hadn't been able to take part in the European War'. The war for Isherwood was a subject of 'all-consuming morbid interest', 'a complex of terrors and longings'. Longing could sometimes outweigh terror as the Orwell–Isherwood generation 'became conscious of the vastness of the experience they had missed'. Hence the fascination of the Spanish Civil War, Orwell goes on, 'was that it was so like the Great War'.

Looking back, C. Day Lewis considered that it was Owen's poetry which 'came home deepest to my generation, so that we could never again think of war as anything but a vile, if necessary, evil'. But this generation was faced with other, apparently greater evils; hence W. H. Auden's 'easy acceptance of guilt in the fact of murder' in his 1937 poem 'Spain'. Owen may have exposed, as Stephen Spender claimed in an essay of the same year, 'the

---

Richard Aldington, *Death of a Hero*; Robert Graves, *Goodbye to All That*; Ernest Hemingway, *A Farewell to Arms*; Ernst Junger, *Storm of Steel*; 1930: Sassoon, *Memoirs of an Infantry Officer*; Frederic Manning, *Her Privates We*.

propagandist lie which makes the dead into heroes in order that others may imagine that death is really quite pleasant', but this revealed truth was not without its own allure. Philip Toynbee, a veteran of the Spanish War, recalls that Owen's poems 'produced envy rather than pity for a generation that had experienced so much'. Keats, the most powerful influence on Owen before his encounter with Sassoon, had declared himself to be 'half in love with easeful death', but Owen had apparently done little to diminish the fear of violent death. 'Even in our anti-war campaigns of the early thirties,' remembers Toynbee, 'we were half in love with the horrors we cried out against.'

The realities of the war, then, were not simply overlaid by an organized cult of Remembrance (Cenotaph, Unknown Soldier, two minutes' silence, poppies, etc.). Rather, our idea of the war, with its elaborately entwined, warring ideas of 'myth' and 'reality', was actively constructed through elaborately entwined, warring versions of memory in the decade and a half following the cessation of actual hostilities.

So it comes about that the war seems, to us, to have been fought less over territory than the way it would be remembered, that the war's true subject is remembrance. Indeed the whole war – which was being remembered even as it was fought, whose fallen were being remembered before they fell – seems not so much to be tinted by retrospect as to have been fought retrospectively.

Owen's famous preface insists that his 'subject is War, and the pity of War' (rather than honour or glory), but his subject might also be termed Memory, and the projection of Memory. His poetry redefines rather than simply undermines Binyon's words ('We will remember them') which also work by projected retrospect. Despite their apparent inappropriateness Owen's poems are now invisibly appended, like exquisitely engraved graffiti, to memorial inscriptions in honour of 'The Glorious Dead'.

In Wanlockhead in north Dumfriesshire, the village memorial takes the form of a mourning soldier atop a marble plinth.

Beneath the statue's feet is written 'Dulce Et Decorum Est Pro Patria Mori', a phrase whose meaning has been wrenched by Owen's poem irrevocably away from the simplicity of the intended sentiment. The old lie has acquired a new ironic truth. By the time Sassoon concludes his 1933 poem 'An Unveiling', a mock-oration for London's 'War-gassed victims', the Latin has been so Owenized as to render further satirical twisting superfluous.

> Our bequest
> Is to rebuild, for What-they-died-for's sake,
> A bomb-proof roofed Metropolis, and to make
> Gas-drill compulsory. *Dulce et Decorum est . . .*

R. H. Mottram hoped the *Spanish Farm Trilogy* might be seen as 'a real Cenotaph, a true War memorial'; Richard Aldington wanted *Death of a Hero* to stand as 'a memorial in its ineffective way to a generation' – but it was only Owen who succeeded, as Sassoon, Blunden, Graves and the rest could not, in memorializing the war in the image of his work. The perfect war memorial – the one which best expresses our enduring memory of the war – would show men bent double, knock-kneed, marching asleep, limping, blind, blood-shod. Either that or – and it amounts to the same thing – it should be a statue of Owen himself.

Owen addressed the issue of his own legacy in 'Anthem for Doomed Youth', a poem which anticipates the time when it will stand as the response to its own appeal: 'What passing-bells for these who die as cattle?' Sassoon made a vital contribution here, substituting 'Doomed' for 'Dead' in an earlier draft so that his friend's poem, like Binyon's, is about those who *are going to have died*. Blunden wrote a poem entitled '1916 seen from 1921' – Owen had written a dozen poems like that four years earlier.

The final line of 'Anthem for Doomed Youth' refers to the

custom of drawing down household blinds as a sign of mourn-ing – of displaying loss – but it is also a disquieting image of concealment, of the larger process whereby the state and the military hid their culpability from scrutiny. These blinds stayed firmly down until Cabinet papers and War Office records became available to researchers in the sixties. Only in the last couple of years, however, have we learnt how Haig, for example, in another telling instance of the way the war seems to have been fought retrospectively, systematically rewrote his diary to make his inten-tions accord with – and minimize his responsibility for – what actually resulted from his command. Denis Winter, whose con-troversial endeavours have cast damaging light on the way the state colluded in perpetuating Haig's preferred version of events, concludes that 'the official record of the war – political as well as military – [was] systematically distorted both during the war as propaganda and after it, in the official history'. The amount of material he has unearthed in Canadian and Australian archives also emphasizes how effectively documents passed on to the Public Record Office in Britain had been 'vetted so as to remove those which contradicted the official line'. Even when the blinds are raised, the sudden rush of light reveals how much is – and will remain – concealed, missing.

Winter's obsessive scrutiny of the Haig records and their incriminating gaps has destroyed the last shreds of Haig's repu-tation; with Owen a similar process has been under way in the opposite direction. His manuscripts have been scrutinized by Jon Stallworthy so that almost every variant of every line is now available. The work of no British poet of this century has been more thoroughly posthumously edited and preserved or, despite Yeats famously excluding him from the *Oxford Book of Modern Verse* (on the grounds that 'passive suffering is not a theme for poetry'), more widely anthologized. In the twenties Haig's reputation was embalmed in an official vacuum of secrecy; like-wise, nothing was known of Owen's life or his development as a poet. In his 1920 edition of Owen's poems Sassoon declared

34

that aside from the poems any 'records of [Owen's] conversation, behaviour or appearance, would be irrelevant and unseemly'. Until Blunden's edition – which included a memoir and what have since become well-known extracts from the letters – he seemed, in Philip Larkin's phrase, 'almost a spirit called into being by the Great War's unprecedented beastliness to assert compassion and humanity'. His poems 'existed for some ten years in a vacuum, as if they were utterances of The Spirit of the Pities in some updated *The Dynasts*'.*

In the early twenties everything about the war – except the scale of loss – was suspended in a vacuum which all the memorials and rites of Remembrance were in the process of trying, in different ways, to fill. Husbands, sons, fathers were missing. Facts were missing. Everywhere the overwhelming sense was of lack, of absence. Overwhelmingly present was 'the pall of death which hung so sorrowful, stagnant and static over Britain'.

To a nation stunned by grief the prophetic lag of posthumous publication made it seem that Owen was speaking from the other side of the grave. Memorials were one sign of the shadow cast by the dead over England in the twenties; another was a surge of interest in spiritualism. Owen was the medium through whom the missing spoke.

They are going to have died: this is the tense not only of the poems of Owen (who carried photos of the dead and mutilated in his wallet) but also of photographs from the war. Although he was thinking only of photographs, both are, in Roland Barthes' phrase, 'prophecies in reverse'. With this in mind, like Brodsky contemplating photographs of Auden, 'I began to wonder

* In the course of writing the review of Stallworthy's biography from which both these quotations are taken, Larkin took the opportunity, in a letter, to offer a succinct opinion of the much more detailed picture of Owen we now have: 'W. O. seems rather a prick, really, yet the poems stay good. A brave prick, of course. You wouldn't catch me waving a revolver at 30 Germans and getting the M C thereby. But not the sort of poetic Angel of Mons (Somme rather) of legend.'

whether one form of art was capable of depicting another, whether the visual could apprehend the semantic.'

It is difficult, now, to imagine the Great War in colour. Even contemporary poems like Gurney's 'Pain' depict the war in monochrome:

> Grey monotony lending
> Weight to the grey skies, grey mud where goes
> An army of grey bedrenched scarecrows in rows...

'I again work more in black and white than in colour,' Paul Klee noted on 26 October 1917. 'Colour seems to be a little exhausted just now.' Many photographs – like those from the first day of the Somme – were taken under skies of Kodak blue, but, even had it been available, colour film would – it seems to us – have rendered the scenes in sepia. Coagulated by time, even fresh blood seems greyish brown.

Photos like this are not simply true *to* the past; they are photos *of* the past. The soldiers marching through them seem to be tramping through 'the great sunk silences' of the past. The photos are colour-resistant. They refuse to come out of the past – and the past is sepia-tinted. Peter Porter in his poem 'Somme and Flanders' notes how 'Those Harmsworth books have sepia'd'; Vernon Scannell in 'The Great War' refers to the 'sepia November' of armistice.

And if, as Gilbert Adair has suggested, Auden's poems of the thirties are somehow 'in black and white', then Owen's, by extension, are in sepia monochrome. It is impossible to colour them in; like photographs, they too are colour-resistant.

> Having seen all things red,
> Their eyes are rid
> Of the hurt of the colour of blood for ever.

In Blunden too 'vermilion', 'damask', the 'pinks and whites' of roses and 'golden lights' of daisies are out of place:

> ... the choice of colour
> Is scarcely right; this red should have been duller.

The world had had the colour bombed out of it. Sepia, the colour of mud, emerged as the dominant tone of the war. Battle rendered the landscape sepia. 'The year itself looks sepia and soiled,' writes Timothy Findley of 1915, 'muddied like its pictures.'

This is why – to return to an earlier theme – the photographs of men queuing up to enlist seem wounded by the experience that is still to come: they are *tinted* by the trenches, by Flanders mud. The recruits of 1914 have the look of ghosts. They are queuing up to be slaughtered: they are already dead.

This characteristic sensation – Larkin's 'MCMXIV' begins with a photo of 'long uneven lines' of men queuing up to enlist – is articulated by Owen in 'The Send-Off', a poem describing recruits about to entrain for France:

> Down the close darkening lanes they sang their way
> To the siding-shed ...

The landscape they leave in these first two lines is a premonition of the one 'a few' may return to, 'up half-known roads', in the last. At the moment of departure they are already marching through the landscape of mourning. The summer of 1914 is shadowed by the dusk of drawn blinds. Before boarding the train they have joined the ranks of the dead:

> Their breasts were stuck all white with wreath and spray
> As men's are, dead.

But Owen's poem does not, so to speak, stop there. The train pulls out into a future that seems, to us, to stretch away from the Great War and extend to the memory of another, more recent holocaust:

> Then, unmoved, signals nodded, and a lamp
> Winked to the guard.

37

So secretly, like wrongs hushed-up, they went.
They were not ours:
We never heard to which front these were sent.

'Agony stares from each grey face.'

Relative to the scale of the slaughter, very few pictures of the
British dead survived the Great War.* This was due principally
to restrictions on reporting. Only official photographers were
allowed at the front; ordinary press photographers were almost
totally excluded from the battle areas; front-line soldiers themselves were discouraged from carrying cameras (or keeping
diaries).

Any photographs that *did* get taken were subject to strict
censorship so that no images prejudicial to the war effort found
their way into print. After the war the archives were vetted so
that the number of photographs of British dead was whittled
down still further†. Like all the most efficient restrictions, these

* This contrasts sharply with the American Civil War; T. H. O'Sullivan's 1863
photograph, 'A Harvest of Death', for example, showed the fields of Gettysburg
strewn with dead.
† In an early visit to the Imperial War Museum photographic department I
began to suspect that this 'cover-up' was continuing into the present day.
Photos from the Great War are catalogued by subject and, despite extensive
filings under 'Destruction', there was no classification for 'Dead' or 'Injured'
or any other heading I could think of. By chance I came across a photo of a
dead soldier. Beneath it was typed, 'Transferred to Casualty Album'. In red
handwriting another note read: 'Not for sale or reproduction'. Having established the correct generic term I moved back to the subject catalogues, but –
as I thought – there was no Casualty Album.
Feeling certain that I had stumbled upon a classic example of the missing-
file conspiracy I explained to one of the assistants, in tones of baffled innocence,
that I couldn't seem to find the so-called Casualty Album.
'Ah, the Casualty Album,' he said. 'It's next door. I'll get it for you right
away, Mr Dyer.' The injunction in red, it turns out, dated from the twenties
so that relatives of the dead would not come across photographs of mutilated

38

successive measures worked consensually rather than simply repressively. Reflecting, establishing and perpetuating a broad agreement between state, photographers and public as to what fell within the limits of acceptable taste, they defined that which they claimed to be defined by.

The pictures that have been preserved show isolated or small groups of dead soldiers. They give no sense of death on the scale recorded by a German Field Marshal on the Eastern Front:

In the account book of the Great War, the page recording the Russian losses has been ripped out. The figures are unknown. Five million, or eight? We ourselves know not. All we do know is that, at times, fighting the Russians, we had to remove the piles of enemy bodies from before our trenches, so as to get a clear field of fire against new waves of assault.

On the Western Front, months after the Battle of the Somme had ended, John Masefield wrote how the dead still 'lay three or four deep and the bluebottles made their faces black'.

Photographs of the missing are themselves missing.

Typically, pictures from the front line show not the dead, but people who have witnessed death. Like this well-known photograph (page 40) of a soldier suffering from battle fatigue. What does this face express? It is difficult to say because any word of explanation has to be qualified by its opposite: there is the most intense appeal for compassion – and an utter indifference to our response; there is reproach without accusation; a longing for justice and an indifference to whether it comes about.

We stare at the picture like Isabelle Rimbaud – sister of the poet – who, in August 1914, took water to a group of exhausted soldiers coming out of battle. 'Where do they come from?' she wondered. 'What have they seen? We should greatly like to know, but they say nothing.'

---

loved ones in the morning paper. It had long since been waived; stored separately as a gesture of decorum the file itself was on my desk within minutes of asking for it.

What has he seen?

This picture, too, is mute. It is immune to our gaze. We are looking into the eyes of a man who has seen the untellable.

In a letter written on the last day of 1917 Owen wrote to his mother 'of the very strange look' he had noticed on soldiers' faces at Etaples. It was, he said,

an incomprehensible look, which a man will never see in England . . . It was not despair or terror, it was more terrible than terror, for it was a blindfold look, without expression, like a dead rabbit's.

It will never be painted, and no actor will ever seize it. And to describe it, I think I must go back and be with them.

Looking across the Channel before he did exactly that, Owen quoted a favourite passage from Rabindranath Tagore: 'When I go from hence, let this be my parting word, that what I have seen is unsurpassable.' Owen's poems are overwhelmingly concerned with this, the fact of having seen:

... As under a green sea, I saw him drowning

In all my dreams, before my helpless sight,
He plunges at me, guttering, choking, drowning.

He had come to France to help his men, he said, by leading them and 'indirectly by watching their sufferings that I may speak of them as well as a pleader can'. In so doing he affirms, repeatedly, his reliability as a witness:

I saw their bitten backs curve, loop, and straighten,
I watched those agonies curl, lift, and flatten.

He focuses frequently – as in the passage from 'Insensibility' quoted above – on 'the blunt and lashless eyes' of men he has seen, men who have been blinded by what they have seen:

O Love, your eyes lose lure
When I behold eyes blinded in my stead!

'O sir, my eyes – I'm blind – I'm blind, I'm blind!'
Coaxing, I held a flame against his lids
And said if he could see the least blurred light
He was not blind; in time he'd get all right.
'I can't,' he sobbed. Eyeballs, huge-bulged like squids',
Watch my dreams still ...

The anger in his poems always comes from this: from the fact of having witnessed what civilians at home could never conceive of seeing. This reaches its most intense expression in the transitional passage in 'Dulce et Decorum Est':

If in some smothering dreams you too could pace
Behind the wagon that we flung him in,
And watch the white eyes writhing in his face ...

Owen, the best-known poet of the First World War, wrote that he was 'not concerned with Poetry'. Robert Capa, the best-known photographer of the Second, declared that he was 'not interested in taking pretty pictures'. During the Spanish Civil War he took the most famous war photograph of all time, which showed – or purported to – the precise moment of a Republican soldier's death in action. In his photographs of the Second World War we come across the dead almost casually, in houses and streets. A photograph from December 1944 shows a frozen winter scene with bare trees, cattle and huts in the background. A GI advances across the photo towards a body lying in the middle of the field. Some way off, beyond the margins of the frame, in the next photograph, there will be another body. Through Capa's photos, in other words, we follow a trail of bodies. This trail leads, ultimately, to the photos of mass death at the core of our century: bodies piled up in concentration camps. Capa, personally, had no intention of photographing the concentration camps, because they 'were swarming with photographers, and every new picture of horror served only to diminish the total effect'.

Theodor Adorno said famously that there could be no poetry after Auschwitz. Instead, he failed to add, there would be photography.

Since the concentration camps we have seen hundreds, thousands of photographs of the dead: from Cambodia, Beirut, Vietnam, Algeria, Salvador, Sarajevo. After the Second World War the work of Capa – an invented name anyway – came less to suggest an individual's work and, increasingly, to identify the kind of photograph associated with him. The original dissolved into the hundreds of reproductions that came in his wake. Photographs of the dead are now ten a penny. More and more news bulletins come with the warning that some of the images in them might upset some viewers. Not only is ours a time when anyone – from Presidents of the United States to nameless peasants – might die on film; this has been the time when, to a degree, people *only* die on film. Like many people I have seen hundreds of bodies on film and never one in real life: an exact reversal of the typical experience of the Great War.

The drift of photography since then has been from looking into the eyes of men who have seen death to seeing things *through* their eyes.

A real photograph of my mother's father: in profile, astride a horse, about to take water up to the front. In another frame, crammed between the glass and a photo showing him standing easy, are four medals. On one, attached to a rainbow-coloured ribbon, is written: THE GREAT WAR FOR CIVILISATION 1914–1919. Another, with a ribbon of fading orange-yellow stripes and blue edges, shows a figure on horseback cantering over a skull. Looking at these medals, I get the impression they were given away willy-nilly: souvenirs to ensure that no one went away empty-handed and everyone had something to show for their pains.

CERTIFICATE OF EMPLOYMENT DURING THE WAR
(Army form Z.18)

Regtl. No. *201334* Rank: *Pte*
Surname: *Tudor*
Christian name in full: *Geoffrey*
Regt: *KSLI*
Regimental Employment – Nature of: *Transport* [the next word is illegible].
Trade or calling before Enlistment: *Farm Labourer*
Course of Instruction and Courses in Active Service Army Schools, and certificates, if any: *nil*
Special Remarks: This is required as a help in finding civil employment: *Steady and reliable. A very good groom and driver. Takes great care of his animals.*
Signed by: *Major* [name illegible]

The history of my family is the history of certificates like this.

Steady and Reliable – these are the qualities which have distinguished us through two world wars.

My father was given a similar reference before he was made redundant from the Gloster Aircraft Company after the Second World War. Years later, when he was made redundant again (aged sixty), he was once more commended for the reliability and steadiness he had displayed over twenty years.

'Takes great care of his animals.' The Major who filled out this certificate might have been *describing* an animal. 'Steady and reliable' – like a dog. Go and find a job with that. Go out into the world with my blessing.

Certificates played their part in enabling me to dispense with the qualities displayed by my father and grandfather. I left school and headed to Oxford with my A Level certificates and my top-of-the-class references. I graduated without being given a certificate proving I had even been there. I had entered a way of life in which certificates and recommendations were silently and invisibly assumed and so could be dispensed with.

My deepest sense of kinship with my family is activated by this form of my grandfather's – not just my love: my class feeling, my ambition, my loyalty. That form – army certificate Z.18 – is why this book has the shape – the form – it does.

*'Tenderness: something on animals and pity,
something on tenderness . . .'*

In footage and photographs of the war there are horses everywhere. So many of them it is easy to think you are watching an early Western, set in an especially dismal period of the American Civil War. In St Jude's Church, Hampstead, there is a memorial to the 375,000 horses killed in the war. In *All Quiet on the Western Front*, after an artillery barrage, the air is full of the screams of wounded horses. The belly of one of them is ripped open. He becomes tangled in his intestines and trips, stumbles to his feet again. 'I tell you,' says one of the soldiers, 'it is the vilest baseness to use horses in the war.'*

The cries that fill the air are worse than those of men who 'could not cry so terribly'. The soldiers 'can bear almost anything'; but this, claims the narrator, Paul, in a passage that anticipates Picasso's *Guernica*, 'is unendurable. It is the moaning of the world, it is the martyred creation, wild with anguish, filled with terror, and groaning.'

The role of horses in memorials has historically been to raise St George above the clutches of the dragon or to hoist the victorious general to a more commanding height above the claims of the everyday. In either case the horse serves as an additional pedestal.†

In Chipilly, on the Somme, the Memorial to the 58th (London) Division by H. Gauquié is of a soldier and his wounded horse. The horse's legs have collapsed, its eyes are rolling in panic. The soldier has one arm around the horse's neck; with the other he strokes its jaw, using his forearm to support its thrashing head. It takes all the soldier's strength to comfort the wounded horse but his lips touch its face as tenderly as a lover's. Both seem about to sink into the stone mud beneath them.

'A very good groom and driver. Takes good care of his animals.'

The driver tends the wounded horse he has led into war. Describing himself as 'a herdsman' and 'a shepherd of sheep', Owen tended his men like 'a cattle-driver'. In action the soldiers 'herded from the blast / Of whizz-bangs' before dying 'as cattle'.

---

* The contrary view is put forward in Cormac McCarthy's novel *All the Pretty Horses*: 'He spoke of his campaigns in the deserts of Mexico and he told them of horses killed under him and he said that the souls of horses mirror the souls of men more closely than men suppose and that horses also love war. Men say they only learn this but he said that no creature can learn that which his heart has no shape to hold.'

† The last equestrian statue to be erected in London was of Earl Haig, in 1934.

45

'And the poor horses . . .' – Constantine

Widespread in writing from the war, the image of the officer as
shepherd and Other Ranks as sheep is especially suggestive, notes
Paul Fussell, 'when the Other Ranks are wearing their issue
sheepskin coats with the fur outside'. As so often happens in the
war, reality runs ahead of metaphor: in 1917 regiments of the

French army marched to the front *baa*-ing like lambs on their way to the slaughter.

Earlier in the same year Sassoon had noted that troops on their way to France seemed 'happy in a bovine way ... They are not "going out" to *do* things, but to have things *done* to them.' In almost identical terms Wyndham Lewis considered that Hemingway had depicted a new kind of man brought into being by the war, a man who 'lives or affects to live *submerged*. He is in the multitudinous ranks of *those to whom things happen* – terrible things, and of course stoically borne.'

Three quarters of a century later, similar impressions are articulated in a larger historic context by Benedict Anderson:

The great wars of this century are extraordinary not so much in the unprecedented scale on which they permitted people to kill, as in the colossal numbers persuaded to lay down their lives. Is it not certain that the numbers of those killed greatly exceeded those who killed?

It is a suggestion confirmed and reinforced by the *way* these numbers met their deaths. Sixty per cent of casualties on the Western Front were from shell-fire, against which shelter was the infantryman's only defence. Artillery fire transformed the foot soldier from an active participant in conflict to an almost passive victim of a force unleashed randomly around him. 'Being shelled,' Louis Simpson claimed later, 'is actually the main work of an infantry soldier.'

Even the artillery officers who dispensed death were tools in the hands of the war machine, calibrating and adjusting something whose destructive might was inbuilt and pre-determined. The real aggressor was industrial technology itself. 'One does not fight with men against *matériel*,' the French commander-in-chief, Pétain, was fond of saying; 'it is with *matériel* served by men that one makes war.'

If shelling meant that courage would increasingly consist of endurance rather than gallantry, the introduction of gas condemned the soldier to a state of unendurable helplessness. Once an enemy gun emplacement had been knocked out, the danger from that source ceased immediately. Once a gas attack had been launched, all soldiers – even those who had initiated it – were simply at the mercy of the elements.

The first lethal gas, chlorine, was an inefficient weapon compared with phosgene and mustard gas which came later. Urinating in a handkerchief and breathing through it – as Robert Ross persuades his men to do in Timothy Findley's novel *The Wars* – was often protection enough. Against mustard gas – which attacked the skin and eyes as well as the lungs – no protection was available. Since it could not be evaded, resisted or fled from, it eliminated the possibility not only of bravery but of *cowardice*, the dark backing which heroism, traditionally, had depended on to make itself visible.

Mustard gas was designed to torment rather than kill. Eighteen times more powerful than chlorine, phosgene was invisible and lethal – but effective masks soon became available. For their survival, then, soldiers were at the mercy of the same industrial technology that was evolving new means of destroying them.

The pattern for the century had been set: the warrior of tradition becomes little more than a guinea pig in the warring experiments of factories and laboratories. Cowering becomes heroism in passive mode. The soldier of the Great War comes increasingly to resemble the civilian sheltering from aerial attack in the Second. 'The hero became the victim and the victim the hero.' Men no longer waged war, it has often been said; war was waged on men. It therefore made no difference if the early zest for war had, by the autumn of 1916, begun to exhaust itself; by then the conflict had acquired an unstoppable momentum of its own.

All of which tempts us to forget that, in spite of Anderson's suggestion, the boys marching off to die for their country were hoping to *kill* for their country. We have become so accustomed to thinking of the slaughter of the war that we forget that the slaughtered were themselves would-be slaughterers. For all their abhorrence of war the poets of protest like Owen, Sassoon and Graves continued – for very different reasons – to wage it. Dominic Hibberd has pointed out how the official citation for Owen's Military Cross refers to his having 'personally manipulated a captured enemy M[achine] G[un] . . . and inflicted considerable losses on the enemy'; in the *Collected Letters* Owen's family offer a milder rewrite of the citation, in which he 'personally captured an enemy Machine Gun . . . and took a number of prisoners'. Sassoon seems to have oscillated between bouts of frenzied violence and bitter loathing of the war that unleashed this strain in him. Graves recalls that he 'had never seen such a fire-eater as [Sassoon] – the number of Germans whom I killed or caused to be killed could hardly be compared with his wholesale slaughter'.

As is so often the case, Barbusse was the first to offer protest in major imaginative form at not simply the suffering the war inflicted on men, but at men's capacity, in time of war, to inflict suffering on others. In 'Dawn', the final chapter of *Under Fire*, a soldier sums up himself and his fellows as 'incredibly pitiful wretches, and savages as well, brutes, robbers, and dirty devils'. A little later one of the group of 'sufferers' says simply: 'We've been murderers.' Together the group of suffering murderers cries 'shame on the soldier's calling that changes men by turn into stupid victims or ignoble brutes'.

when
Will kindness have such power again?

One of the reasons for the war's enduring power is the way that, in the midst of so much brutality and carnage, compassion and kindness not only failed to wither but often flowered.

The most moving episodes in the war always involve the awakening of a sense of the enemy's shared humanity. Often this is initiated by the simplest gesture – an enemy soldier offering prisoners cigarettes or a drink from his canteen. On Christmas Day 1914 there was a truce along the whole length of the Western Front. In some circumstances, especially where the gap between the two lines of trenches was small, this became tacitly extended into the 'live and let live' policy whereby each side refrained from antagonizing the other. 'For either side to bomb the other,' Charles Sorley had realized as early as July 1915,

would be a useless violation of the unwritten laws that govern the relations of combatants permanently within a hundred yards of distance from each other, who have found out that to provide discomfort for the other is but a roundabout way of providing it for themselves.

Most poignant of all are the occasions when tenderness springs directly from an appalled awareness of the pain inflicted on the enemy. A German battalion commander recalls that after the British began their retreat from the battlefield at Loos in September 1915, 'no shot was fired at them from the German trenches for the rest of the day, so great was the feeling of compassion and mercy for the enemy after such a victory.'

Henry Williamson remembers coming across

a Saxon boy crushed under a shattered tank, moaning 'Mutter, Mutter, Mutter,' out of ghastly grey lips. A British soldier, wounded in the leg, and sitting nearby, hearing the words, and dragging himself to the dying boy, takes his cold hand and says: 'All right, son, it's all right. Mother's here with you.'

Episodes like these are scattered throughout memoirs and oral testimonies from the war. Civilians bayed for blood and victory; combatants, meanwhile, had become passive instruments of their nations' will. In the words of Arthur Bryant:

German civilians sang specially composed hymns of hate against England and, in the most civilized country in the world, quiet inoffensive English gentlemen and ladies who had never seen a blow struck in anger scouted the very mention of peace and spoke of the whole

German race as they would of a pack of wild beasts. Only in the battle-line itself was there no hatred: only suffering and endurance: death and infinite waste.

In *Under Fire* the shattered survivors of French and German units sleep side by side in the mud. This moment of exhausted solidarity is then worked up into the climactic vision of fraternity in which war will have no place. The experience of the trenches gives rise to Barbusse's socialist-pacifist vision of a possible future. In this light the mutinies that rocked the French army in the spring of 1917 were like grumbling premonitions of revolution. The mutinies were suppressed, discipline was restored, conditions – food, leave – were improved. A similar configuration of experience, however, could lead to a more violently protracted form of discontent as there emerged from the conflict 'men whom the war had ruined ... who incorporated the renovating ideals of the socialist tradition, the cult of the earth, the taste of violence that had grown in the mud of the trenches.'

'That was a laugh,' remarked a German soldier on being told the war was over. 'We ourselves are the war.'

In London the Armistice Day ceremonies of 1921 had been disrupted by a demonstration by the unemployed, whose placards read: 'The Dead are remembered but we are forgotten.' In one of his *Last Poems*, published posthumously in 1932 (the year after Blunden's edition of Owen), D. H. Lawrence presents a prophetic vision of the deepening depression and political unrest of the thirties as an expression of the 'disembodied rage' of the dead who died in vain, who 'moan and throng in anger'. Never explicitly identified with the war, these 'unhappy dead' are yet impossible to disassociate from it. Set on a 'day of the dead' in November, the poem makes it seem as if the army of the surrogate dead that marched past the Cenotaph has now joined the massed ranks of the disillusioned, the unemployed, the dispossessed. The war that was to end all wars will lead inexorably to another, a world made safe for democracy seethes with this betrayal of the discontented dead:

> Oh, but beware, beware the angry dead.
> Who knows, who knows how much our modern woe
> is due to the angry, unappeased dead
> that were thrust out of life, and now come back at us
> malignant, malignant, for we will not succour them.

In the face of unemployment, inflation and the other indignities and privations of peacetime, the shared suffering of the trenches offered an almost mythic embodiment of total belonging: the immersion of the individual within a rigidly hierarchical community of equals. For the movement that articulated this ideal in Germany, peace was a continuation of the war by means which, ultimately, led to its full-scale resumption after a simmering twenty-year interlude.

Sassoon had noted how soldiers became almost happy in the knowledge that they were abandoning their own volition to the directives of the army; Nazism subsumed the individual will to the will of the Reich, the Führer. An ideological imperative was built from the martial ideal of obedience which the army had instilled in its soldiers.

'The Third Reich comes from the trenches,' said Rudolf Hess. But so too does the end of the idea of obedience as unequivocally heroic. A British survivor of the Somme remembers how

the war changed me – it changed us all ... Everybody ought to have this military training. It would do them good and make them obedient. Some of the young men now, they need obedience. They don't know what it is. Our lives were all obedience.

The passage contains its own implicit contradiction, yielding where it seeks to uphold, tacitly acknowledging that it was precisely the experience of the Great War that brought obedience and servitude into tainted proximity. Henceforth obedience

would have some of the qualities of submission and complicity –
culminating, for victims and perpetrators alike, in the Holocaust – and all heroism would have about it some of the quality
of refusal, rebellion and – a key term in the next war – *resistance*.
D. H. Lawrence had noticed this submissive quality of courage
among recruits in Cornwall: 'They are all so brave, to suffer,' he
wrote in July 1916, 'but none of them brave enough, to reject
suffering.'

Perhaps the real heroes of 1914–18, then, are those who
refused to obey and to fight, who actively rejected the passivity
forced upon them by the war, who reasserted their right not to
suffer, not to have things done to them.

Which is why, despite a series of diversions, wrong turnings
and U-turns, I made such an effort to find the village of
Bailleulmont.

In the communal cemetery there, tucked away from the tangle
of civilian graves, is a group of military headstones. Unusually,
they are made of brown stone, on one of which is inscribed:

10495 PRIVATE
A. INGHAM
MANCHESTER REGIMENT
1ST DECEMBER 1916

SHOT AT DAWN
ONE OF THE FIRST TO ENLIST
A WORTHY SON
OF HIS FATHER

Like over 300 others, four of the soldiers buried here in
Bailleulmont were shot for desertion or cowardice. Two of
them – Ingham and Alfred Longshaw – were friends who served
together – at the Somme – deserted together, were executed
together and now lie together. For years Ingham's family believed
he had simply 'died of wounds' – as the inscriptions on the
headstones of other executed men maintain – but when his

father was informed of the truth he insisted on this inscription being added to the headstone.

A campaign was recently mounted to have executed deserters pardoned. A letter printed in the *Independent* provides a vivid illustration of the extent to which our idea of heroism has changed:

My father was highly decorated in the First World War – DSM, MM and three times mentioned in dispatches. But his greatest pride was in the time when, escorting a deserter to death at dawn, he let him escape. This was not a latterday judgement, but that of one who had been involved in all the perils of the front line, and lost a limb in the process.

The deserter's grave has become a hero's grave; pride has come to reside not in the carrying out of duty but in its humane dereliction.*

'I've seen 'em, I've seen 'em . . .'

The war goes on, silently, visibly. The same faces, the same ground. Men march up to the front, waving steel helmets. Artillery barrages. Lots of carrying: ammunition, shells, supplies. Larking around in the trenches. Lunch. More marching. More artillery. The attack. The first few prisoners brought in. The odd casualty. The landscape taking a pounding (with special emphasis on mine craters). A rubbled village. Walking wounded returning. Troops coming back with prisoners, miserable shaven-headed Hun . . .

I am in the Imperial War Museum, watching a compilation of documentary films from the war. Each film seems identical to all the others. Their form is as fixed as the gridlock of trenches in which they are set.

---

* On 15 May 1994 a memorial inscribed 'To all those who have established and are maintaining the right to refuse to kill' was unveiled in Tavistock Square, London. The inscription continues: 'Their foresight and courage give us hope.'

The camera stops everything. Soldiers can't keep their eyes off it. During a pre-battle service no one listens to the padre: everyone is too busy watching the camera. Watching and grinning. The war is a grinning contest which the allies are winning (Jerry can only muster a weary smile). Only the most badly wounded – whom we never actually see – can resist grinning at the camera. Being so camera-conscious gives rise, inevitably, to some strikingly bad acting. Never more so than in the famous faked sequence of troops apparently going over the top in *The Battle of the Somme* (first shown, to a public horrified by its realism, on 21 August 1916) which was actually filmed at a training ground. A soldier falls, dies, looks back to the camera and then folds his arms neatly across his chest.

The smoking, by contrast, is entirely convincing. At any time at least half the people in shot are puffing away. They smoke so much you suspect they are trying to build up resistance to possible gas attacks. To our eyes these films are vintage cigarette ads – especially since a good proportion of these smokers are only days or hours away from getting blown to bits and so the possibility of developing lung cancer in twenty years is a luxurious pipe-dream. Still, what with smoking, gas, artillery, noise, damp and generally poor conditions of hygiene and sanitation, war, in these films, seems characterized by a general disregard for the health of the soldier.

All the more remarkable, then, that nothing too serious results from it. Gilbert Adair has pointed out that in Hollywood films of the Vietnam War 'every American character who happens to find himself within the camera's field of vision is *already* in danger'. In this documentary view of the First World War the camera frame is a safe haven, a refuge from danger. To be on film is to be out of harm's way.

Hardly anyone dies and they're all Germans anyway. As for the Tommies they have the odd arm wound, sometimes a head bandage, usually just a limp. After the battle friend and foe alike tramp back together – Tommy supporting Fritz – as if from a fiercely contested rugby match in atrocious conditions. After the game it's all handshakes, friendliness and slapstick fraternization: a British soldier changes hats with a German prisoner (the title reads 'Tommy and Fritz change hats'). Everyone looks on. All in all the battles of the Somme and Ancre look pretty harmless affairs.

Harmless and, from an allied point of view, entirely successful. The role of the German army is to suffer terrible bombardment and then surrender in numbers so vast the whole army must have been rounded up by 1917 at the latest.

So it goes on. Everyone looks the same. Everywhere looks the same. Every battle looks the same. And so, while titles and maps give an impression of a succession of easy victories, the films undermine themselves: if it's all so straightforward, why this need to fight another identical battle, over an identical patch of ground a few months later? What we end up with is, as Samuel Hynes almost accurately puts it,

masses of men and materials, moving randomly through a dead ruined world towards no identifiable objective; it is aimless violence and passive suffering, without either a beginning or an end – not a crusade, but a terrible destiny.

Destiny is the wrong word here, for it implies a purpose, a goal, and thereby contradicts his main point that 'nothing really *happens*'. Not a destiny, then, but a *condition*.

After a couple of hours of this condition I am stupefied by boredom. My interest is revived briefly by a sequence showing an officer in cavalry uniform – cap, boots, riding coat, *riding* a tank. An innovation so novel that on titles the word is always flanked by inverted commas, the 'tank' is the real star of these films. Ugly, slow, it lumbers up to the battlefield and then lumbers back again, unscathed and terrifying, an ungainly iron beetle. A bucking beetle, an iron bronco rather, for as it dips and grinds over the cratered field the officer perched atop tries desperately to keep a stiff upper body.

After this humorous interlude the war reverts to the plodding, plotless norm. The same faces, the same ground. I imagined I could watch footage endlessly and am surprised by my longing for modern documentary framing, for the raw material of history to be recut, edited down further, reshaped and contextualized. I almost find myself wishing there were a few of those interviews with ageing generals ('Yes, I like to think I did for them both with my plan of attack.') that I'd hated in *The World at War*.

The war goes on, silently, visibly. The same faces, the same ground. A title says something about our tireless armies marching without rest and I feel I'm the tireless viewer yomping without pause through the battles of Ancre, the Somme, Arras – I've long stopped noticing which is which or taking notes. I sit for another quarter of an hour, slumping deeper and deeper in my chair. Eventually I can bear it no longer. I get up, bang on the projectionist's door and plead, 'O Jesus, make it stop!'

He is only too happy to call a truce. He can knock off a bit early for lunch too. Live and let live. As I walk out I half expect to be presented with a white feather by more diligent researchers.

This is what the war is like for us. We can stop it at will. We gaze at photographs of soldiers in the trenches. Snow, dirt, cold, death. When we have been there long enough, we get up and leave, turn the page and move on.

The war was filmed at 16 to 18 frames per second on hand-cranked cameras. Modern projectors – like the one in the museum's screening room – run at 24 frames per second and so the action flickers quickly by.

As part of an installation in the museum's main building a special projector has been set up to show an endless loop of parts of *The Battle of the Somme* at the correct speed. Men marching to the front, survivors limping back. This is the middle segment of that continuous line of men first seen entraining for France and glimpsed later winding its way past the Cenotaph. An endless loop: a river of men, moving towards death. They are dead and they are going to die. Marching to the front, endlessly, so slowly that they never cease marching. In Craiglockhart, Sassoon remembered the war in an almost identical image:

I visualized an endless column of marching soldiers, singing 'Tipperary' on their way up from the back areas; I saw them filing silently along the ruined roads, and lugging their bad boots through mud until they came to some shell-hole where trees were stumps and skeletons . . .

Because the original cameras were hand-cranked, it is imposs-ible to synchronize the projector exactly. Consequently the action is often slower than it should be. Like a photo taken at a shutter speed so slow it actually moves, the picture 'ghosts'.

'The past is never dead,' wrote William Faulkner. 'It's not even past.'

Before going over the top, an officer said that his men 'seemed more or less in a trance'. Charles Bean, the official Australian historian of the war, noted that after action 'the men appeared to be walking in a dream and their eyes looked glassy and starey'. Another survivor recalls going through battle 'like a sleepwalker'. David Jones notes of combat-weary soldiers that 'they come as sleepwalkers whose bodies go unbidden of the mind, without malevolence, seeking only rest'.*

In Manning's *The Middle Parts of Fortune*, a company of men are about to march to the front to join a major offensive on the Somme. The men looked at each other 'with strange eyes, while the world became unreal and empty, and they moved in a mystery, where no help was'. When the order to move off is given there comes

a rippling murmur of movement, and the slurred rhythm of their trampling feet, seeming to beat out the seconds of time, while the liquid mud sucked and sucked at their boots, and they dropped into that swinging stride without speaking . . . and the mist wavered and

* In another evocative phrase a few pages later Jones writes of 'fog-walkers'.

trembled about them in little eddies, and earth, and life, and time, were as if they had never been.

In one of the best passages in his memoirs, Sassoon watched an exhausted Division *returning* from an offensive on the Somme:

Now there came an interval of silence in which I heard a horse neigh, shrill and scared and lonely. Then the procession of returning troops began. The camp-fires were burning low when the grinding, jolting column lumbered back. The field guns came first, with nodding men sitting stiffly on weary horses, followed by wagons and limbers and field-kitchens. After this rumble of wheels came the infantry, shambling, limping, straggling and out of step. If anyone spoke it was only a muttered word, and the mounted officers rode as if asleep. The men had carried their emergency water in petrol-cans, against which bayonets made a hollow clink; except for the shuffling of feet, this was the only sound. Thus, with an almost spectral appearance, the lurching brown figures flitted past with slung rifles and heads bent forward under basin-helmets.

Sassoon was 'overawed' by what he had witnessed; it seemed as though he 'had watched an army of ghosts'. In that characteristic wartime attitude of projected retrospect Sassoon felt he 'had seen the war as it might be envisioned by some epic poet a hundred years hence'. Almost ninety years later this film is the epic, endless poem of the war.

Bearing a wounded comrade over his shoulder, a soldier floats towards the camera. Silent, ghostlike, slow.

Watching the sleep-walking figures we enter dream time, dead time: the remembered dreams of the dead.

A river of men, flowing towards death. Marching to the front, endlessly. Survivors limping back, lessly.

One thing emerges plainly from all this footage: war, for the ordinary soldier, was a continuation of labouring by other means. The battlefield was a vast open-air factory where hours were long, unions not permitted and safety standards routinely flouted.

It thereby combined the worst aspects of agricultural labour and industrial shiftwork. The 'mysterious army of horsemen, ploughmen and field workers who', in Ronald Blythe's words, 'fled the wretchedness of the land in 1914' discovered, in Flanders, an intensification of wretchedness. Miners found themselves engaged in exactly the same activity they had pursued in peacetime – except here their aim in burrowing beneath the earth was to lay hundreds of pounds of high explosive beneath the enemy's feet. The Germans, meanwhile, were engaged in similar operations and sometimes the two tunnel systems broke through to each other. Hundreds of feet beneath the earth 'men clawed at each other's throats in these tunnels and beat each other to death with picks and shovels'.

For those above ground the chief activity recorded on film is carrying. Before the battle, shells; after, stretchers. Life, one realizes, is primarily a question of loading and unloading, fetching and carrying. Many of the shells are too heavy to be lifted and have to be winched or rolled into position. Every piece of equipment looks like it weighs a ton. There were no lightweight nylon rucksacks or Gor-tex boots. Things were made of iron and wood, even cloth looks like it has been woven from iron filings. Everything weighed more then. Weighed down with equipment, men do not march to the front so much as carry themselves there. Greatcoats are not worn but lugged:

> We marched and saw a company of Canadians,
> Their coats weighed eighty pounds at least.

This is one of the lessons of history: things get lighter over time. The future may not be better than the past but it will certainly be lighter. Hence the burden, the *weight* of the past.

We feel this especially strongly when looking at the memorial sculptures of Charles Sargeant Jagger. Some sculptors coax stone into a deceptive lightness; Jagger emphasizes its heaviness.

In the 1907 relief *Labour* (since destroyed) men strain and sweat to shift a piece of equipment; one figure in the right-hand corner seems exhausted, injured or wounded. Only the slightest addition of detail would be necessary to render the scene suitable for use as a relief on Jagger's best-known work, the Royal Artillery Memorial at Hyde Park Corner.

We stopped there one night in August. Obscured by trees, isolated for most of the day by a moat of traffic, no one else in the car even knew the memorial was there. There were four of us, all drunk. It was two in the morning and still warm. Moonlight

The weight of the past

glanced off the black figures. We looked up at the figure lugging shells, his gaze fixed blankly into the future or the past or whatever it is that the present eventually becomes.

'Men became reminiscent and talkative as they looked at the

figure carrying four 18-pound shells in the long pockets of his coat,' reported the *Manchester Guardian* the morning after the memorial was unveiled on 18 October 1925.

He would perhaps carry them a long distance, they said, if the gun was camouflaged, and like as not he would have two more under his arms. It meant a great weight added to the 96 pounds of an artillery man's equipment.

Dead weight

Even in rest the weight of their equipment drags down on the men. We walked around the memorial, sheltered from the noise of the traffic. At the side of the memorial a figure lay covered by a greatcoat, part of his face — an ear, the line of his jaw — just visible. He is simply *dead weight*.

Jagger's distinctive style combines this almost hulking heaviness of stone and equipment with the most delicate of details: you can almost see the hairs on the shell-carrier's forearms, hear the rustle of the letter read by the soldier waiting at Paddington station. A scarf wrapped around his neck, a greatcoat draped around his shoulders, absorbed in the act of reading. The promise and dread of letters. Propped against the bar of the Café de

Charles Sargeant Jagger: memorial at Paddington station

l'Industrie, I open an envelope with my name in your writing. The second paragraph wonders, in your latest flourish of colloquial English, how I am 'bearing up'.

The scale and strength of Jagger's figures recall the heroes of classical sculpture, but they are utterly ordinary. His sculptures are of average men whose heroism lies in their endurance. Jagger himself was shot through the left shoulder in Gallipoli in November 1915; in April 1918 he was again badly wounded at the Battle of Neuve Eglise. On both occasions he made a speedy recovery: 'I heal,' he wrote in May 1918, 'almost before I've been hit.' What he emphasizes in his sculpture is not the body's vulnerability but its resilience, its capacity for bearing up. His figures – most obviously in the Hoylake and West Kirby Memorial, or in the identical maquette 'Wipers' at the Imperial War Museum – stand their ground, guarding their own memory. Their backs are, typically and literally, against the wall.

Public sculpture aims to display itself to maximum effect. There is an inherent difficulty, therefore, in using as the basis for such sculpture figures whose main aim was the exact opposite: maximum concealment. During the day, front-line troops stayed below ground level; only under cover of darkness or during a major offensive did they venture out into the open. Rather than revealing itself on a plinth, then, an authentic figure should, except on rare occasions, seek cover behind or – ideally – beneath it.

Like almost all of Jagger's figures the Artillery officers are sheltered and protected by their own Memorial. Only the hunched machine-gunners of Jagger's Portsmouth Memorial are framed by open air.

Jagger may have been the best but he was not the only sculptor to benefit from the needs of Remembrance. Commissions for most of the British memorials in France were given to architects but at home the post-war period represented a boom period for sculptors. For French sculptors times were even better. Thirty thousand war memorials – or fifty a day – were raised in France between 1920 and 1925. 'There hasn't been a golden age like this since the Greeks, since the cathedrals,' says a memorial sculptor in Tavernier's film *Life and Nothing But*. 'Even the most ham-fisted sculptor is inundated with commissions. It's like a factory production line. Talk of the Renaissance, this is the Resurrection.'

Inherently backward-looking, sponsored, mainly, by the state and the military, Memorial art will always tend to the conservative rather than experimental – even more so when the war to be commemorated has early on identified 'tradition' with England and home, 'modern' with the enemy. By implication 'traditional' figurative sculpture was readily compatible with victory, or at least with the milder affirmation that the war had not been utterly devoid of purpose. By similar and paradoxical implication, modernism – in the post-war years which witnessed its consolidation and triumph – seemed to identify itself with defeat or, more mildly, with hostility to the values in whose name the war had been waged.

Significantly, the principal modernist memorials were designed in Germany, the defeated nation, by Ernst Barlach and Käthe Kollwitz (both of whose work was subsequently condemned by the Nazis).

In Britain, memorials were executed in the main by older, more established sculptors like Albert Toft (1862–1949) and William Goscombe John (1860–1953). Even the major commissions undertaken by younger sculptors like Walter Marsden (1882–1969), Gilbert Ledward (1888–1960) and Jagger himself (1885–1934) were cast in traditional forms.

'Survivor outrage' – as James Young terms it – was also a factor determining the essentially conservative nature of memorials. As representatives of the dead, survivors tend to be hostile to abstract representation of their past: 'Many survivors believe that the searing reality of their experiences demands as literal a memorial as possible.' Such public hostility to the experimental or abstract is not always wrong-headed or philistine. The memorials of Toft and Jagger have endured better than less traditional works, like those of Edward Kennington for example. Over time his simple totemic forms, crowded on to a plinth in Battersea Park, have been unable to perform the basic function of the Memorial: to give shape to the past, to contain it.

And yet, from this confluence of needs and socio-aesthetic

forces there emerges the possibility of a memorial sculpture which, in Britain at least, never came into existence, which is missing from the art historical record: a wounded realism, a sculpture rooted in a figurative tradition but maimed by modernism; a memorial sculpture which is both rent asunder and held together by the historical experience it seeks to express. Such a memorial form might have resembled Zadkine's *Monument to Rotterdam*, or Ernst Neizvestny's *Soldier Being Bayoneted*. These were made in the 1950s but both use 'a sculptural language which derives from the same period of the early 1920s'.

A work from slightly earlier, Wilhelm Lehmbruck's haunting *The Fallen* of 1915–16, shows that sculptural language beginning to express itself in terrible sobs. A naked, painfully etiolated figure is on his hands and knees. His head hangs to the floor. The grief of Europe seems to bear down on his back but this fallen youth is still supporting himself, resisting the last increment of collapse (his head touches the floor but this sign of helplessness adds to the sculpture's structural stability). Another work by Lehmbruck, *Head of a Thinker*, shows a figure whose arms appear to have been wrenched off, leaving the shoulders as rough stumps; the left hand is clenched against the chest from which it protrudes. Lehmbruck worked as an orderly in a military hospital in Berlin and was devastated by the injuries and suffering he witnessed. He committed suicide in 1919, but his work might have provided a model for future memorials.

Similar works – better ones, sculptures stripped of Lehmbruck's tendency to implicitly elide the suffering of the artist with that of the fallen soldier – could have forced themselves into existence in the inter-war years in Britain. Alternatively, given that the figurative sculptural tradition is inherently heroic, the possibility existed for a realist sculpture which showed the suffering of war more nakedly than ever before: a group of men advancing and falling in the face of machine-gun fire, stretcher-bearers floundering in mud ... Sculptures do show injured soldiers but the wounds tend to be heavily formalized, hindering rather than maiming. The sculptural representation of slaughter exists only in a bas-relief by Jagger. Now in the Imperial War Museum, *No Man's Land* of 1919–20 shows a sprawling wilderness of men dying and wounded, one of whom hangs crucified from barbed wire.

That such an explicit depiction of battle was nowhere given fully three-dimensional expression highlights another absence – especially if the bas-relief as a form is considered as the bronze or stone equivalent of a photograph, as a static tracking shot. While they could convey the aftermath of action, it was physically impossible for photographers to capture battle itself (one of the reasons the sequence of soldiers going over the top at the Somme is obviously faked is precisely *because* it was filmed); as a medium sculpture was capable of rendering the unphotographable experience of battle. Although many had the talent, no British sculptor – not even Jagger – had the vision, freedom or power to render the war in bronze or stone as Owen had done in words.

This speculative account of sculptures that were not made is really only an attempt to articulate a sense of what is missing from those that *were*: a way of describing them in terms not of stone or bronze but of the time and space which envelop and define them. What is lacking is the sense of a search for a new form, a groping towards new meaning rather than a passive reliance on the accumulated craft of the past.*

* Eventually, perhaps, the experience of the war did find expression in the most representative work of a sculptor whose distinguishing characteristic was, precisely, the elision of the figurative and the abstract. Henry Moore joined the army in 1916, when he was eighteen. He served as a machine-gunner and was gassed at Cambrai in November 1917. After being hospitalized for two months, he became an instructor in bayonet drill. Anthony Barnett has hinted at the significance of this experience for the 'sculptor who discovered the hole'. More generally, Barnett suggests that it is Moore's experience of the war that 'vividly explains, and is expressed by, the terrible stare and the crippled posture shared by his reclining figures'. If Moore's reclining men were scattered over a landscape, we would be 'at the site of a massacre'. Barnett's argument is subtle and provocative rather than trenchant or definitive. He is at pains to point out that while Moore's characteristic work 'must be seen as in some way

Even taking this absence into account, the realist memorials represent a great flowering of British public sculpture. That they may not have been the work of exceptional individual talents illustrates how, at certain moments in the tradition of any art, the expressive potential of the average can exceed that of the outstanding at earlier or later dates. Nowadays the human form cannot so readily be coaxed into such powerful attitudes; only an exceptional artist today could achieve the power routinely managed by the memorial sculptors, almost all of whom, except Jagger, have been forgotten.

We drive through Keighley on our way to watch Leeds–Everton at Elland Road. Clouds hug the ground. The anorak, a foreigner would suppose, is the English national dress. The most frequently heard noise is a sniff. Everything that is not grey – clouds, road, pigeons – is brown: benches, buildings, leaves, bronze soldier and sailor, the figure of Victory perched on the memorial behind them. Traffic and shoppers hurry past. The soldier stands erect, doing his best to ignore the fact that the bayonet on his rifle has long been broken off.

In Bradford, too, where we stop for a lunchtime curry, the bronze soldiers have met a similar fate. Once they must have strode aggressively forward, one each side of the memorial. Now they advance gingerly, as if about to surprise each other in a harmless game of hide and seek. That the bayonet was already virtually obsolete as a weapon by 1914 – 'No man in the Great

---

incorporating [his war] experience' it cannot be 'reduced to a response to the war'. Moore's work should be contrasted with memorials which, typically, view the war as 'a tragic eruption into an otherwise pleasant society'. As noted, war, for working-class soldiers, was a continuation of labour by other means, an amplification and intensification of the misery inflicted by mine and factory. Moore was a miner's son and he responded to the war not with protest but as 'a witness to a way of life that at one moment found expression in mass-warfare'. The condition of his figures is one of resignation to forces that overwhelm but can never crush them.

War was ever killed by a bayonet,' claimed one soldier, 'unless he had his hands up first' – only enhances the lack. Then as now the bayonets' function was symbolic and ornamental: without them the sculptures' internal dynamic is thrown irremediably out of kilter.

In Holborn, by contrast – or, more quietly, in the French village of Flers, where there is an almost identical figure – an infantryman mounts a pedestal of land, rifle in hand, encircled by the vast radius of air that extends from head to bayonet-tip to trailing foot. This framing circle renders the sculpture (by Albert Toft) both more powerful and more vulnerable, extending his command of space and fixing our attention, as if through a sniper's sights, on the soldier at its dead centre.

Near Huddersfield, in Elland, the light has called it a day. Twilight is falling through the bare trees. November here can last ten months of the year. The damp grass is covered in damp leaves. On a granite plinth a bronze soldier keeps watch in a drizzle of mist, looking out at the damp road. The collar of his greatcoat is turned up against the coming cold. Old rain drips from the rim of his helmet. Except for the verdigris streaking his shoulders, all colour is a shade of grey. Brodsky:

> Leaning on his rifle,
> the Unknown Soldier grows even more unknown.

At Stalybridge a soldier slumps into death. His body crumples beneath him but an angel is there; she has been waiting, it seems, for exactly this moment. Berger has described another almost identical memorial in a village in France:

The angel does not save him, but appears somehow to lighten the soldier's fall. Yet the hand which holds the wrist takes no weight, and is no firmer than a nurse's hand taking a pulse. If his fall appears to be lightened, it is only because both figures have been carved out of the same piece of stone.

They are all over the country, these Tommies ...

Elland Memorial

They are all over the country, these Tommies: taking leave of their loved ones (in Newcastle), standing to, resting, reading letters, attacking (in Kelvingrove Park near Glasgow), binding their wounds (in Croydon), helping injured comrades (in Argyll), dying, returning home (to Cambridge). Representing and preserving a sample of the multitudinous gestures of the British soldier at war, these frequently duplicated poses put me in mind of the Airfix soldiers which moulded my taste in memorial art.

Age may not weary them but the years have condemned. Sun-dozed and snow-dazed, they sweat in greatcoats in the summer or freeze in shirtsleeves through the long winter months. Sprayed by feminists – 'Dead Men Don't Rape' – and damaged by vandals, all are rotted by pollution. Powerless to protect themselves, their only defence, like that of the blind, is our respect.

Sometimes they are the only old things in the new No Man's Land of bankrupt businesses and boarded offices, broken lifts and derelict estates. They have been around so long they seem part of the landscape: it is impossible to imagine a time when they were not here. For years now, children who watched the statues being unveiled have been dying of old age. Perhaps what they commemorate, then, is their own survival, the enduring idea of remembrance. The most common form of sculpture – a soldier, head bowed, leaning on his downward-pointed rifle – actually represents the self-contained ideal of remembrance: the soldier

The self-contained ideal of remembrance

being remembered and the soldier remembering. Sculptures like this appeal to – and are about – the act of remembrance itself: a depiction of the ideal form of the emotion which looking at them elicits.

Throughout the 1920s, and especially in the early thirties, attempts were made to ally the rituals of Remembrance with the cause of peace: war memorials, it was argued, should be termed peace memorials; white 'peace' poppies were sold by the Peace Pledge Union as an alternative to the red poppies of the British Legion. Already, by 1928, however, the public was beginning to cease thinking of itself as 'Post-War' and was beginning, in the words of a contemporary commentator, 'to feel that it was living in the epoch "preceding the next Great War"'. But this was exactly the period when the Great War was being remembered – in novels and memoirs – most intensely. Again there is a strange temporal elision as the idea of Remembrance merges into a notion of Preparedness. Accordingly, sculptures erected in memory of the First World War come also to look forward to the Second. As war with Germany looms again, the memorial sculptures come to represent a form of symbolic rearming whose job is not simply to protect the past but to guard against possible futures.

On the Croydon memorial P. J. Montford's figure bandages a wound as if in readiness for further exertions; in Port Sunlight two fit men – sculpted by William Goscombe John – prepare to defend a third who is wounded; John Angel's figure in Exeter and Walter Marsden's in St Anne's on Sea show soldiers weary but ready (if necessary the rifle that was broken in victory in one sculpture will be wielded as a club in this one).

Jagger's figures lent themselves particularly well to the new conditions in which remembrance merged into resolve. Resisting suggestions that any peace symbolism be included in the Royal Artillery Memorial, he had emphasized that the 'terrific power' of the artillery represented the 'last word in force'. This, he had insisted, was a *war* memorial.

On the south coast, in Portsmouth, Jagger's machine-gunners were already in place. As plans were made to entrench ourselves in our island stronghold, the weary Tommies became sculptural equivalents of the Home Guard: men from an earlier war whose effectiveness was largely symbolic. This time it was not gallant Belgium but Britain itself that had to be protected – and these figures became everyday reminders of Britain's resolve to stand firm. Battered but resilient, they were visible prefigurements of Churchill's determination to fight invaders at every street corner.

In 1944 the Guards Division Memorial in St James's Park was badly damaged by a German bomb. The sculptor Gilbert Ledward thought this improved it because 'it looked as though the monument itself had been in action'. When the Ministry of Works got round to repairing it, Ledward suggested that some 'honourable scars of war' be allowed to remain – a way of registering how, in memorializing one war, his monument had participated in another.

Sculpted by Philip Lindsey Clark, the Southwark War Memorial in Borough High Street shows a soldier striding forward. Soon after it was unveiled, this photograph was taken. Few other images contain so much time.

The statue preserves or freezes a moment from the war. This record itself ages, very slowly. Since it was taken, both the statue and the photograph itself have aged. Looking at it now, what we see is an old photograph of a new statue. In the background, gazing at the camera, are four men and a boy. The long exposure time has caused these figures – who moved slightly – to ghost, especially the two on the right whom we can see right through. Any figures walking past will have vanished completely. Because it is utterly still, the statue itself is substantial and perfectly defined – all the more strikingly so given that it shows an infantryman moving purposefully forward. The photograph is therefore a record of time *passing*: both in relation to the statue (which, relative to the people looking at it, is fixed in time) and through it (because the statue itself no longer looks quite as it does in the photograph). Compared with the solid permanence of the memorial, even the buildings in the background seem

Time

liable to fade. What we see, then, is the sculpture's own progress through time; or, more accurately, time as experienced *by* the sculpture. Simultaneously, the old time of the onlookers, this moment of vanishing time, is preserved in the picture which records its passing.

—

In a few days we will be leaving for Flanders. Mark tells me he has been reading Trevor Wilson's huge history, *The Myriad Faces of War*, as preparation. I am impressed and a little shamed by his diligence. My own reading of general histories of the war is characterized by a headlong impatience. Basil Liddell Hart, A. J. P. Taylor, John Terraine, Keith Robbins – I read them all in the same inadequate way. With a cloudless conscience I skim the same parts of each: the war at sea, air raids on London, anything happening on the Eastern Front, Gallipoli … Then there are the parts of these histories I try hard to concentrate on but whose details I can never *absorb*: the network of treaties, the flurry of telegrams and diplomatic manoeuvres that lead up to the actual outbreak of war. Consequently everything between the assassination of Archduke Ferdinand and the lamps going out over Europe is a blur.

Although I always dwell on the period of enthusiastic enlistment, I move attentively but fairly quickly through the period 1914–15. It is not until the great battles of attrition that I am content to move at the pace of the slowest narrative. From the German offensive of 1918 onwards I am once again impatient and it is not until November, the armistice and its aftermath, that the speed of history and my reading of it are again in equilibrium.

For me, in other words, the Great War means the Western Front: France and Flanders, from the Somme to Passchendaele. Essentially, then, mine is still a schoolboy's fascination. Uncertain of dates and eager for battles, I pause again over a passage I had marked years before, when I *was* a schoolboy, in Leon Wolff's *In Flanders Fields*:

… a khaki-clad leg, three heads in a row, the rest of the bodies submerged, giving one the idea that they had used their last ounce of strength to keep their heads above the rising water. In another miniature pond, a hand still gripping a rifle is all that is visible, while its next door neighbour is occupied by a steel helmet and half a head, the staring eyes glaring icily at the green slime which floats on the surface at almost their level.

All of which is of no interest except in so far as my own interests coincide with the remembered essence of the conflict. Is it not appropriate and inevitable that I should move quickly through the period of the war's relative mobility before getting stuck into every detail of the stalemate of 1916–17? Rather than being a quirk of temperament, perhaps this is how the war insists on being remembered, on *remembering itself* . . .

After meeting him in Craiglockhart in August 1917, Owen began immediately and consciously to absorb the influence of Sassoon. Enclosing a draft of the poem 'The Dead-Beat', Owen explained in a letter how, 'after leaving him, I wrote something in Sassoon's style'. Sassoon also lent Owen a copy of *Under Fire*, which he read in December. Sassoon took a quotation from Barbusse's novel as an epigraph for *Counter-Attack* and Owen used passages as the basis of images in his poems 'The Show' and 'Exposure'.

If Owen found it helpful to see his own experience of the war through first Sassoon's and then Barbusse's words, it has since become impossible to see the war except through the words of Owen and Sassoon. Literally, since so many books take their titles from one – *Remembering We Forget*, *They Called it Passchendaele*, *Up the Line to Death* – or the other – *Out of Battle*, *The Old Lie*, *Some Desperate Glory* – of them. Owen's lines in particular offer a virtual index of the themes and tropes featured in these books: mud ('I too saw God through . . .'); gas ('GAS! Quick, boys!'); 'Mental Cases'; self-inflicted wounds ('S.I.W.'); the 'Disabled'; homoeroticism ('Red lips are not so red . . .'); 'Futility' . . .

So pervasive is his influence that a poem about the Second World War, Vernon Scannell's 'Walking Wounded', seems less an evocation of an actual scene than a verse essay on Owen. Owen's 'stuttering rifles' rapid rattle' becomes the 'spandau's manic jabber' (the rhythmic similarity enhanced still further by the Owenesque near rhyme of 'jabber' and 'rattle'). The wounded, when they enter, look like they have tramped straight out of 'Dulce et Decorum Est':

> Straggling the road like convicts loosely chained...
>   ... Some limped on sticks;
> Others wore rough dressings, splints and slings...

Scannell was aware of this; as Fussell points out, he even wrote a poem about how 'whenever war is spoken of', it is not the one he fought in but the one 'called Great' that 'invades the mind'.

The difficulty for recent novelists is that the same thing also happens when they are dealing with the Great War itself.

Recent novels about the war have the benefit of being more precisely written, more carefully structured than the actual memoirs, which tend, with the magnificent exception of *All Quiet on the Western Front*, to be carelessly written and structured. Robert Graves' *Goodbye to All That*, Richard Aldington's *Death of a Hero*, Guy Chapman's *A Passionate Prodigality*, Frederic Manning's *The Middle Parts of Fortune* (also known as *Her Privates We*) and Sassoon's *The Complete Memoirs of George Sherston* all contain impressive passages, but none has the imaginative cohesion of purpose and design or the linguistic intensity and subtlety to rival the English translation of Erich Maria Remarque's masterpiece.*

---

* Many of these books only attracted the attention they did in the wake of the renewed interest in the war generated by the phenomenal success of *All Quiet*. In May 1929 Richard Aldington sent a telegram to his American agent: 'Referring great success Journey's End and German war novels urge earliest fall publication Death of a Hero to take advantage of public mood. Large scale English war novel might go big now.'

The problem with many recent novels about the war is that they almost inevitably bear the imprint of the material from which they are derived, can never conceal the research on which they depend for their historical and imaginative accuracy. Their authenticity is mediated; they feel like secondary texts. In 1959 Charles Carrington complained that certain passages in Leon Wolff's *In Flanders Fields* read like 'a pastiche of the popular war books which everyone was reading twenty-five years ago'. Thirty-five years on, Wolff's evocative historical study of the Flanders campaign is likely to be a major source book for anyone wishing to fictionalize the war. We have, in other words, entered the stage of second-order pastiche: pastiche of pastiche.

In the Afterword to the 1989 edition of *Strange Meeting* (the title is, of course, from Owen), her novel about the friendship that develops between two English officers at the front, Susan Hill notes that as well as immersing herself in memoirs and letters, she had, in writing her book, to make 'an imaginative leap' and 'live in the trenches'. Though successful in its own terms, this leap is over-determined by the material amassed in the run-up to it. Especially in the sections of the novel which try to pass themselves off as unmediated primary sources – the letters supposedly written by David Barton, the younger of the two central characters.

Well there [he writes to his mother], I have told you what it's like and made it sound bad because that is the truth and I would have you believe it all, and tell it to anyone who asks you with a gleam in their eye how the war is going. A mess. That's all ... Tell all this to anyone who starts talking about honour and glory.

We have noticed a tendency, during the war, to look forward to a time in the future when the participants' actions could be looked back on; here is the opposite process of historic back-projection. Barton's letters fail to ring true – not because he would not have expressed sentiments like this, but because, ironically, they correspond so exactly with those established as the historical legacy of the war. Their authenticity derives from exactly the process of temporal mediation they have, *as letters*, to disclaim. In this instance it is difficult not to recall the famous passage from *A Farewell to Arms* in which Hemingway established the template for Barton–Hill's sentiments:

I was always embarrassed by the words sacred, glorious, and sacrifice and the expression in vain ... Abstract words such as glory, honor, courage, hallow were obscene.

In a later letter Barton observes, parenthetically, that if British soldiers are attending to the wounded, the Germans 'often hold their fire ... as we do'. Again, it is the verifiability of the observation that renders its dramatic authenticity suspect. Barton's remark is the product, we feel, not of the contingency of his own experience but the judiciousness of Hill's research.

The imaginative fabric of Sebastian Faulks' impressive war novel *Birdsong* absorbs the research so thoroughly that only a few of these leaks appear. Faulks' own observation, that one of his characters 'seemed unable to say things without suggesting they were quotations from someone else' nevertheless has ironic relevance to some passages in the book. Just back from leave, an officer gives vent to his loathing of the civilians living comfortably back in England: 'Those fat pigs have got no idea what lives are led for them,' he exclaims. 'I wish a great bombardment would smash down Piccadilly into Whitehall and kill the whole lot of them.' An entirely authentic sentiment, but one too obviously derived from a famous letter of Owen's (see p. 29 above) to ring *individually* true.

Given the near impossibility of remaining beyond the reach of Sassoon and Owen, one solution is to include them in the fictive world of a novel. Pat Barker has done exactly this in two fine novels, *Regeneration* and *The Eye in the Door*. Set in Craiglockhart, the former opens with a transcription of Sassoon's famous declaration and dramatizes many of the crucial moments in his relationships with Dr W. H. R. Rivers and Owen (including his detailed amendments to early versions of 'Anthem for Doomed Youth').

Unlike Hill, Faulks and Barker, Eric Hiscock actually served in the war and saw action near Ypres in the spring of 1918. Born in 1900, he did not publish his memoir *The Bells of Hell Go Ting-a-ling-a-ling* until 1976, six years after the first edition of *Strange Meeting*. The fact that he has no gifts as a writer makes his case more revealing. On one occasion he notes that the

ever-present dreamlike quality of the days and nights (nights when I heard men gasping for breath as death enveloped them in evil-smelling mud-filled shell-holes as they slipped from the duckboards as they struggled towards the front line) filled me with an intense loathing of manmade war.

Reality recedes with each 'as' until the final heartfelt declaration can barely sustain the weight of its own conviction. Even moments of extreme personal danger are rendered secure and comfortable by the familiar conventions by which they are expressed. 'Terrified, I clawed the stinking mud as the bullet whistled round my head and shoulders and I waited for death.' The whole war is compressed into a single cliché.

In *The Bloody Game* (another Sassoon-derived title) Fussell mentions that some have considered Hiscock's memoir 'not as factually accurate as it pretends to be'. Whether it is a true account is not the issue here. What is important is that, for Hiscock, the linguistic and thematic conventions of the genre are more powerful than the original experience; indeed the original experience can only be revealed by the accretion of clichés it is buried beneath. The homely crudity of Hiscock's language makes him *more* – not less – susceptible to mediated expression. A lack of linguistic self-consciousness exacerbates the tendency to express the experience of war through the words of others. Hiscock unwittingly acknowledges this when, as a way of adding resonance to an incident, he concludes by observing 'if that wasn't a theme for Siegfried Sassoon, I don't know what was'. In terms of the writing that results from his experiences Hiscock may as well not have participated personally in the events of his own story.

The problems built in to Hill's naturalist novel and Hiscock's memoir disappear in a book like Timothy Findley's *The Wars*, which heightens the linguistic and narrative strategies on which it depends. The problem of mediation is resolved by accentuating it. The novel's superb setpieces – in which the protagonist Lieutenant Ross shoots an injured horse in the hold of the troopship, becomes lost in Flanders fog, or shelters from a gas attack – seem wholly authentic because Findley avails himself of the full range of narrative gambits which have become available in the years since the war. Hill's characteristic register is a vaguely twenties literary English; Findley's jagged self-enhancing fragments anticipate the technique of Michael Ondaatje's Second World War novel, *The English Patient*. Ross's sensations are recorded with a linguistic resourcefulness that is nowhere achieved in the memoirs. After a deafening barrage, to pick the tiniest of examples, Ross's 'ears popped and the silence poured in'.

The structure of the book incorporates and depends on the research that has gone into its writing: transcripts of interviews, letters, old photographs ... 'What you people who weren't yet born can never know,' reads one such transcription,

is what it meant to sleep under silent falls of snow when all night long the only sounds you heard were dogs that barked at trains that passed so far away they took a short cut through your dreams and no one even awoke. It was the War that changed all that. It was. After the Great War for Civilization – sleep was different everywhere ...

Findley moves, often within the space of a couple of paragraphs, from the contingencies of a moment-by-moment present tense to the vast historical overview. Instead of an imaginative leap into the trenches, in other words, he enters the time of photographs. Sometimes, when there is no 'good picture available except the one you can make in your mind', present and past, description and speculation resolve into each other. The staple tropes of the front are reinvented:

The mud. There are no good similes. Mud must be a Flemish word. Mud was invented here. Mudland might have been its name. The ground is the colour of steel. Over most of the plain there isn't a trace of topsoil: only sand and clay. The Belgians call them 'clyttes', these fields, and the further you go towards the sea, the worse the clyttes become. In them, the water is reached by the plough at an average depth of eighteen inches. When it rains (which is almost constantly from early September through to March, except when it snows) the water rises at you out of the ground. It rises from your footprints – and an army marching over a field can cause a flood. In 1916, it was said that you 'waded to the front'. Men and horses sank from sight. They drowned in mud. Their graves, it seemed, just dug themselves and pulled them down.

No eyewitness account is more evocative than this, precisely because Findley acknowledges that the most vivid feature of the Great War is that *it took place in the past.*

It therefore takes an effort of considerable historical will to remember that before the war Thiepval, Auchonvillers and Beaumont-Hamel were just places like any others, that the Somme was a pleasant river in the *département* of the same name. But in 1910, in Faulks' *Birdsong*, when Stephen Wraysford arrives at Amiens, that is all it is, a place – where he falls for the wife of the local factory-owner with whom he is lodging. They are consumed by passion, but brooding over the doomed love affair is the greater doom that will soon consume the earth beneath their feet.

In the course of their outings they see 'a small train waiting to take the branch line into Albert and Bapaume'. A second train takes them 'from Albert out along the small country line beside the Ancre, past the villages of Mesnil and Hamel to the station at Beaumont'. Another pushes its way south 'where the Marne joined the river Meuse, whose course linked Sedan to Verdun':

a network of innocent connections that will soon define the geography of the Western Front. In Amiens Cathedral Stephen has a vision of the 'terrible piling up of the dead' of centuries, which is also a premonition of what is to come. On oppressive, sultry afternoons husband, wife and lover go punting in the stagnant backwaters of the Somme. Thiepval is a spot to take afternoon tea. The future presses on the lovers like the dead weight of geological strata. The Great War took place in the past – even when it lay in the future.

To us it *always* took place in the past.

The issue of mediation has been compounded by Paul Fussell, who I am reading again as preparation for our trip to Flanders. If it was impossible to write about the war except through Owen's and Sassoon's eyes, it is now difficult to read about it except through the filter of Fussell's ground-breaking investigation and collation of its dominant themes. Whenever we read the war poets, we effectively borrow Fussell's copies to do so and – even when we dissent from his judgements – cannot ignore his annotations and underlinings. Fussell has himself become a part of the process whereby the memory of the war becomes lodged in the present. His commentary has become a part of the testimony it comments on. (Reading him – or anyone else for that matter – I am searching for *what is not there*, for what is missing, for what remains to be said.) If Hill's *Strange Meeting* is an example of primary mediation, then *The Great War and Modern Memory* raises the possibility of secondary or critical mediation.

Even the ceremonies of Remembrance are subject to mediation. Now that the two world wars are commemorated with a service at the Cenotaph on the Sunday closest to the eleventh of November, it is – as the term Remembrance Day suggests – the act of remembering together that is being remembered. Contemporary works like *A Twentieth-Century Memorial* by Michael Sandle (born in 1936) – a skeletal Mickey Mouse

manning, or *mousing*, a bronze machine-gun – are memorials to
the near extinction of the war memorial as a viable form of
public sculpture.

And this book? Like the youthful Christopher Isherwood who
wanted to write a novel entitled 'A War Memorial', I wanted to
write a book that was not about 'the War itself but the effect of
the idea of [the War] on my generation'. Not a novel but an
essay in mediation: research notes for a Great War novel I had
no intention of writing, the themes of a novel without its
substance . . .

I see Ypres and the surrounding area through the words of
Stephen Graham and Henry Williamson . . . We arrive there in
the afternoon darkness and book into an expensive cheap hotel.
There are FIRE EXIT signs on every door, brown covers on the
beds. Towels the size of napkins, burn marks on the dresser. Our
room is the sort which demands that even non-smokers spend
the first conscious minutes of the day propped up in bed, exhaling
smoke at the hangover ceiling.

In the evening we walk to the *Grote Markt*, the vast square in
the centre of town. After Ypres was flattened during the war,
many buildings – like the fourteenth-century Cloth Hall that
dominates the *Markt* – were rebuilt just as they had been. Williamson returned here in 1927 to find Ypres unrecognizably
'clean and new and hybrid-English'. Sixty years of ageing have
given it the look of a pleasant if slightly gloomy somethingth-
century town, scrupulously preserved.

After a couple of beers we make our way to the Menin Gate,
the memorial to the Missing of the Ypres salient. The names
of 54,896 men who died between 1914 and 15 August 1917
are carved here. Designed by Sir Reginald Blomfield, it is a
version of a triumphal arch, so extended as to seem almost like
a tunnel. Steps in the middle of this tunnel take us up to the
outside of the memorial. From here we can see the leafy water

of the canal beyond the Gate. Damp air. Stillness waiting on itself.

We walk back down inside the memorial and then beyond it, across the canal. From this distance the buildings stretching away from the Gate seem to crouch beneath it. And yet, at the same time, it belies its own scale and you wonder if it is really as big as it seems. Everything about the memorial suggests that it should work powerfully on you, but its effect is oddly self-cauterizing.

> Well might the Dead who struggled in the slime
> Rise and deride this sepulchre of crime.

By 1927 when Sassoon scrawled these words – metaphorically speaking – on the recently inaugurated Menin Gate, his tone of maimed derision had become a matter of reflex. If 'this pomp' of 'peace-complacent stone' is a misrepresentation and denial, then so, equally, is Sassoon's response to it. Refusing to accommodate the possibility of atonement for 'the unheroic Dead' on whose behalf he is lobbying, Sassoon yet conveys – and thereby yields to – the memorial's own version of itself when he writes of the 'intolerably nameless names'.

In his novel *Fields of Glory* Jean Rouaud describes life in the kind of 'sullen swamp' that, for Sassoon, is the enduring truth of the Ypres battlefield:

Little by little, abandoned corpses sank into the clay, slid to the bottom of a hollow and were soon buried under a wall of earth. During an attack you stumbled over a half-exposed arm or leg. Falling face to face on a corpse, you swore between your teeth – yours or the corpse's. Nasty the way these sly corpses would trip you up. But you took the opportunity to tear their identification tags off their necks, so as to save those anonymous lumps of flesh from *a future without memory,* to restore them to official existence, as though the tragedy of the unknown soldier were to have lost not so much his life as his name.

Rouaud here affirms the underlying longing that links those 'who struggled in the slime' and the memorial arch on which they are commemorated. Lord Plumer was not bandying empty rhetoric when, at the inauguration of the Gate, he declared on behalf of the bereaved: 'He is not missing; he is here.'

Memorials to the Missing are not about people, they are about names: the nameless names.

It is almost eight o'clock. A few people have congregated beneath the arches. The clocks begin to chime damply. Traffic comes to a halt. Two buglers take up position beneath the Gate and play The Last Post.

The two minutes' silence on the second anniversary of the armistice was broken by The Last Post, 'acute, shattering, the very voice of pain itself – but pain triumphant,' according to *The Times*. In *Death of a Hero* the burial of George Winterbourne is concluded by the same 'soul-shattering, heart-rending ... inexorable chains of rapid sobbing notes and drawn-out piercing wails' that are heard here at the same time every day of the year.

A boy cycles past. One of the buglers gestures quietly for him to stop. The sound of the bugles ricochets from the walls of the memorial. Echoes chase themselves between the arches. The last notes fade away, beckoning into silence. Afterwards silence lies on the dark canal, a silence in which every note is preserved intact.

Traffic resumes. We drift away, eat dinner, drink some more. It is very cold. Perhaps it is just the weather, perhaps it would be different in the summer – though one feels this is the season when the town comes into its own – but Ypres seems, in Stephen Graham's phrase, 'a terrible place still'. Graham was writing about the Ypres of 1920, when 'death and the ruins completely outweigh[ed] the living'. The ruins have been replaced by replicas of the original buildings, there is nothing wrong with the town – though it is not the kind of place you would come for a honeymoon – but you can see what Graham meant when he wrote that

it would be easy to imagine someone who had no insoluble ties killing himself here, drawn by the lodestone of death. There is a pull from the other world, a drag on the heart and spirit.

Especially in our dismal hotel room. We lie on our beds, half pissed. Mark is reading *Death's Men*; Paul, *They Called It Passchendaele*; I read *The Challenge of the Dead*. Eventually the other two drop off to sleep. I go on reading. I 'lie listless, sleepless, with Ypres on the heart, and then suddenly a grand tumult of explosion, a sound as of the tumbling of heavy masonry'.

Paul snoring.

We drive along the flat roads of Flanders through the dregs of autumn. Every crossroads is smeared with tractor mud. It has stopped raining and started to drizzle. 'Intermittent' is the nearest we get to turning off the wipers – the Ypres, as we prefer to call them. The landscape is a sponge, soaking up rain. Turnips or beets – root vegetables of some kind, in any case – are piled up at entrances to fields.

Because the car is rented, we drive at top speed through every puddle and slick of mud, rally-cross style. Soon it is plastered with muck. From now on we refer to it as the tank: 'Let's park the tank', 'The tank needs petrol ...' Mainly, because it is so cold, we say, 'Let's get back in the tank.'

Near St Julien we come to Frederick Chapman Clemesha's Canadian Memorial: the bust of a soldier mounted on and merging into a pillar of square stones. Head tipped forward, facing not towards the enemy lines of old but back towards Ypres. Rain smoking around him, dripping from the brim of his tin helmet. Thin trees in the distance. Sky grey as the rain-streaked stone of the monument.

We are in no hurry to leave. The memorial makes no appeal and no demands. It commands its solemn patch of land. Withstanding rain and time, we stand with it, this imperturbable monument.

Beyond that it is difficult to say what feelings the memorial evokes. Not pity, not pride, not sadness even. Henry Williamson acknowledged this uncertainty while remaining ostensibly

Mourning for all mankind?

untroubled by it. For him it is a 'memorial to all soldiers in the war'. Having found a way of articulating the statue's refusal to yield to an easily identifiable response, he generalizes still further: it 'mourns for all mankind' – at which point the actual statue all but disappears in a fog of generalized emotion. It is a grand gesture and a self-defeatingly banal one: if all mankind is to be mourned, there would be no need to single out for special lamentation this particular

BATTLEFIELD WHERE 18,000
CANADIANS ON THE BRITISH
LEFT WITHSTOOD THE FIRST
GERMAN GAS ATTACKS THE
22–24 APRIL 1915 2,000 FELL
AND LIE BURIED NEARBY

In *Fields of Glory* Jean Rouaud describes a gas attack in terms that recall the rolling fog of *Bleak House* or the slinking catlike fog of Eliot's 'Prufrock':

Now the chlorinated fog infiltrates the network of communication trenches, seeps into dugouts (mere sections of trench covered with planks), nestles in potholes, creeps through the rudimentary partitions of casements, plunges into underground chambers hitherto preserved from shells, pollutes food and water supplies, occupies space so methodically that frantic pain-racked men search vainly for a breath of air.

The leisurely sentence unfolds infinitely slowly, gradually revealing the harm that this apparently harmless stain on the air can do until, finding yourself running out of breath with several clauses still to go, you are suddenly struggling for the full stop. The initial lyrical lilt of the scene is soon rent apart by 'the violent cough that tears the lungs and the pleura and brings bloody froth to the lips, the acrid vomiting that doubles up the body'.

John Singer Sargent's paining *Gassed* shows a line of ten men making their way through the mass of other gas victims sprawling on the ground on either side of them. Their eyes are bandaged and, as in Brueghel's *Parable of the Blind*, each man has his hand on the shoulder of the one in front. In the middle of the group

The only sound . . .

a soldier turns away to vomit. Another, near the front, raises his leg high, expecting a step. An orderly guides and steadies the two men at the head of the line. Further off, to the right of the low sun, another group are making their way uncertainly forward.

The soldiers in the foreground lie sleeping or resting, propped on one another. One drinks from a canteen. In the sky there are planes where birds should be, flying haphazardly.

Henry Tonks, another war artist who was with Sargent when he saw the gassed soldiers, recalls the scene:

They sat or lay down on the grass, there must have been several hundred, evidently suffering a great deal, chiefly I fancy from their eyes which were covered up by pieces of lint.

In *Gassed* there is little suffering. Or rather, what suffering there is is outweighed by the painting's compassion. In spite of the vomiting figure the scene has almost nothing in common with Owen's vision of the gas victim whose blood comes 'gargling from the froth-corrupted lungs'. What Sargent has depicted, instead, is the solace of the blind: the comfort of putting your trust in someone, of being safely led. At the same time the light itself seems enough to restore their sight, light so soft that it will soothe even their gas-ravaged eyes. Pain is noisy, clamorous. In Sargent's painting coughing and retching are absorbed by the tranquillity of the evening. The lyricism at the opening of Rouaud's description is beginning to make itself felt again as air and men convalesce, reasserting their capacity for tenderness.

The scene is already touched, in other words, by the beauty of the world as it will be revealed when their vision is restored.

The only sound, that is ... But no, I am getting ahead of myself.

In the first months of the war football was used as an incentive to enlistment; the war, it was claimed, offered the chance to play 'the greatest game of all'. By the end of 1914 an estimated 500,000 men had enlisted at football matches. By the following spring, professional football had been banned: matches, it was feared, were so popular that (a reversal of the initial strategy) they *deterred* men from enlisting.

At the front the enthusiasm for the game continued unabated. Whether a match actually took place in No Man's Land between German and English troops on Christmas Day 1914 is doubtful; even if it did not, it is entirely appropriate that the day's events should have generated the myth of a football match as the embodiment of fraternization.

The most famous footballing episode was Captain Nevill's kicking a ball into No Man's Land on the first day of the Somme. A prize was offered to the first man to dribble the ball into the German trenches; Nevill himself scrambled out of the trench in pursuit of his goal and was cut down immediately. (Perhaps the Somme was not only an indictment of military strategy but also of the British propensity for the long-ball game.) Lawrence's admonition – that tragedy ought to be a great big kick at misery – could not have been fulfilled more literally.

Move close to Sargent's painting, closer than its size compels. Through the legs of the gassed soldiers – and especially in the gap opened in the line by the vomiting man – you can glimpse a game of football being played in the background. One team in red, the other in blue, the ball in mid-air, suspended in the lovely evening light.

The only sounds not absorbed by the light are the shouts of the game, just audible to the line of blinded men.

Road signs direct us through history as well as geography: Poel-capelle, Zonnebeke, Passchendaele. 'There were many words that you could not stand to hear and finally only the names of places had dignity,' wrote Hemingway in *A Farewell to Arms*. A generation later Philip Toynbee remembers, as a boy, 'murmuring the name '*Passchendaele* in an ecstasy of excitement and regret'. Vernon Scannell too was mesmerized by the 'litany of proper names' which crop up, in various permutations, again and again in his poems: 'Passchendaele, Bapaume, and Loos, and Mons'; 'Cambrai, Bethune, Arras, Kemmel Hill'; 'Passchendaele, Verdun, The Menin Road ...'

I cannot remember when in my childhood I first heard of places like these. But I know I heard them – the Somme especially – at home, before I came across them in history books or at school. It was at the Somme that history engaged my family, that my family entered history. Like Shurdington, Cranham, Birdlip, Leckhampton and Churchdown, the name was part of the soil in which the history of my family was rooted. This intertwining of the villages and landmarks of Gloucestershire with those of Flanders and Picardy is also the defining charac- teristic of the poetry of Ivor Gurney.

Appropriately, his first volume of poetry, published in 1917, was entitled *Severn and Somme*; in the letters and poems he wrote from the trenches, and afterwards in the long years of mental illness, he exclaims again and again how – a source of comfort and torment – the landscape of northern France resembles his beloved Gloucestershire. At Crucifix Corner 'all things said Severn'; in another poem the same spot reminds him of Crickley. Near Vermand, 'the copse was like a Cranham copse with scythed curve', like 'Cotswold her spinnies if ever ...' Hearing a cuckoo in 'a shattered wood ... what could [he] think of but Framilode, Minsterworth, Cranham, and the old haunts of home'. Recalling the time he was gassed at 'bad St Julien' (long after that first attack, in September 1917), the poem 'Farewell' sets the dual landscapes of 'Ypres', 'Somme and Aubers' and 'Gloucester', 'Cheltenham', 'Stroud' swirling around each other.

Gurney was born in 1890 and served in the Gloucesters, the same regiment as my father's father. The last fifteen years of his life were spent at the City of London Mental Home, but when he died, in 1937, he was buried just outside Gloucester. Running

93

past the bottom of our garden, Hatherley Brook passes within half a mile of the church at Twigworth where he is buried.

We drive into Passchendaele. The power of this name has not diminished with the years. As words, 'Auschwitz' and 'Dachau' have become over-burdened by their rhetorical power as synonyms for evil. If not in print then certainly in conversation Belsen has become a common metaphor for extreme skinniness. Passchendaele, despite the carnage associated with it, is rarely heard except to designate the Battle of Third Ypres. Instead of passing into common linguistic currency, then, these place-names have acquired an almost sacred ring. They have perhaps become over-loaded with holiness, especially Passchendaele. For those who were there, Passchendaele was so awful, so horrific, that it became almost a joke. Paul reads aloud the accounts of two survivors quoted by Lyn Macdonald: 'Tuesday, 2 October. Back in the battery again, but what have we come back to? Passchendaele!' Another recalls that

the names were so sinister – Zonnebeke – Hill 60 – Zillebeke – the names terrified you before you got there, they had such a sinister ring about them. Then to end up making for Passchendaele was the last straw.

This tone of disaffected endurance is not confined to place-names.

Paul Fussell sees the war, via Hardy, as a huge 'satire of circumstance' in which irony emerges as the only adequate mode of expression. Hence, he notes satirically, '*The Oxford Book of War Poetry* might just as well be titled *The Oxford Book of Satire.*' The war for Fussell is a text which he has read more perceptively and persuasively than anyone else. The participants are consequently judged in literary terms: Haig is reproved for a 'want of imagination and innocence of artistic culture'; the 'hopeless absence of cleverness' about one of his plans is 'entirely characteristic of its *author*'. In such company 'it is refreshing to turn to a wittier tradition', to Sir Herbert Plumer, for example, 'a sort of intellectual's hero of the British Great War'. Not surprisingly the war demanded from its generals 'the military equivalent of wit and invention' – exactly the qualities so abundantly displayed by a 'sophisticated observer' like Fussell himself. For Fussell, in short, irony is synonymous with sophistication – which makes it especially ironic that the war's most deeply ironic mode is probably the 'mustn't grumble' proletarian grumble. (Sassoon did not simply try to depict the war in realist terms; he tried to find a poetic diction of *moaning*.)

Of the prose writers it is Frederic Manning who – despite a tendency to lop off every aspirate in sight – has best conveyed this pervasive idiom:

'What 'appened to Shem?' [Bourne] asked.
'Went back. Wounded in the foot.'
' 'e were wounded early on, when Jerry dropped the barrage on us,' explained Minton, stolidly precise as to facts.
'That bugger gets off everything with 'is feet,' said Sergeant Tozer.
' 'e were gettin' off with 'is 'ands an' knees when I seed 'im,' said Minton, phlegmatically.

Trench songs like 'The Old Battalion', used to famous effect in *Oh What a Lovely War*, are musical elaborations of exactly this brand of deadpan resignation. First performed by Joan Littlewood's Theatre Workshop in 1963, *Oh What a Lovely War* reached a wider audience in 1969 when it was filmed by Richard Attenborough. I half saw the film a couple of times, but, disliking music hall and the theatre in equal measure, it never made any impression on me. It wasn't until I read it as a text – in wilful defiance, as Sassoon might have put it, of a prefatory note which warns that 'this is a play script and should be read as such' – that I found a version I could respond to. The satirical attacks on Haig and the generals still seem to rely on crude caricature, but the trench scenes contain some of the best writing about the war. Writers may have resorted to irony, but the soldiers here rely on its more humane equivalent: the piss-take.

On Christmas Eve the Germans sing 'Stille Nacht, heilige Nacht'; the British respond with a carol of their own:

> It was Christmas day in the cookhouse,
> The happiest day of the year,
> Men's hearts were full of gladness
> And their bellies full of beer,
> When up spoke Private Shorthouse,
> His face as bold as brass,
> Saying, 'We don't want your Christmas pudding
> You can stick it up your ...'
> Tidings of comfort and joy, comfort and joy ...

In the course of the play almost all of the themes touched on in this book are dealt with in similar style. In place of a meditation on *Gassed* we have:

> They're warning us, they're warning us,
> One respirator for the four of us.
> Thank your lucky stars that three of us can run,
> So one of us can use it all alone.

Listening to 'those poor wounded bleeders moaning in no-man's-land', a soldier notes that it 'sounds like a cattle market'. The literary endeavours of the writer-soldiers – and the birth of the war's written mythology – receive similarly short shrift:

SECOND SOLDIER: What's he doing?

THIRD SOLDIER: Writing to his lady love.

SECOND SOLDIER: Oh blimey! Not again.

THIRD SOLDIER: Third volume. My dearest, I waited for you for two hours last night at Hellfire Corner, but you didn't turn up. Can it be that you no longer love me? Signed – Harry Hotlips.

SECOND SOLDIER: What's she like?

FOURTH SOLDIER: Lovely.

SECOND SOLDIER: Is she?

THIRD SOLDIER: Bet she's got a nose like a five-inch shell.

FOURTH SOLDIER: Shut up will you? I'm trying to concentrate.

FIFTH SOLDIER: You writing for that paper again?

FOURTH SOLDIER: Yes, they don't seem to realize they're in at the birth of the *Wipers Gazette*. Here, do you want to hear what I've written?

SECOND SOLDIER: No.

Appropriately and perfectly, the play ends with a song which, like that defining passage in Barbusse, looks ahead to the impossibility of conveying what happened in the trenches:

And when they ask us, and they're certainly going to ask us,
The reason why we didn't win the Croix de Guerre,
Oh, we'll never tell them, oh, we'll never tell them
There was a front, but damned if we knew where.

Oh What a Lovely War was not 'written' in the conventional sense; it grew out of a close collaboration by all the members of the Theatre Workshop. In a characteristic aside Fussell, by contrast, notes that 'it is really hard to shake off the conviction that this war has been written by someone'. The great value of Lyn Macdonald's books is that they are not texts so much as carefully arranged accumulations of raw material which have not been 'worked up' as they have in *Oh What a Lovely War*. Preserved in *1914* or *Somme* are the voices of men – like my grandfather – who never sought to record their experiences on paper. The tropes identified by Fussell are reproduced in a different, 'lower' or non-literary register which simultaneously qualifies and verifies many of his claims.

Sassoon's observation, in *Memoirs of an Infantry Officer*, that 'the symbolism of the sunset was wasted on the rank and file' suggests that Fussell's elaborate analysis of sunsets has only literary significance – but sunsets bathe the accounts of even the least literary men in a lyric glow. Likewise, Fussell's lengthy examination of the way the war was ironically underwritten by the sporting spirit is both supported by and wrenched away from its Newboltian public school context by an incident recorded by Macdonald. Lieutenant Patrick King, in the midst of shelling, calls across to see if his men are all right. The reply comes: 'Aye, all's reet here, Paddy. We're still battin'.'

This tone of deadpan resignation is surprisingly versatile. It embraces a range of the rhetorical devices catalogued in *The Great War and Modern Memory*. Fussell notes the way that *The Pilgrim's Progress* provided a symbolic map of the war (Passchendaele is the Slough of Despond); one of Macdonald's interviewees begins with the graphically exact understatement, 'The salient was a dead loss,' and moves in ten lines beyond Bunyan to describe it as 'just a complete abomination of desolation'.

This pretty much sums up our feelings about Passchendaele. We buy bread, fruit and pink-coloured meat at a supermarket and then go for coffee. At eleven-thirty in the morning the café is already full of men, beer and smoke.

'To our dismay, on counting our money, we found that it was nearly gone,' noted Williamson in 1927. 'Whither had it gone?'

'We must have spent more on beer than we thought,' suggests Paul before going through the figures in the back of his notebook again. However we look at it, money is pouring through our fingers. After further anguished calculations we put it down to the exchange rate. A few weeks ago the pound plunged to a new record low, and as a consequence we are sitting here in Passchendaele, the poor men of Europe, licking our financial wounds.

We leave the café and head for Tyne Cot Cemetery, a vast, sprawling city of the dead. Like any metropolis it has preserved the haphazard, unregulated heart of the old city: the 300 or so graves that were found here after the armistice. Since then it has spread out in a series of radial fans and neat purpose-built suburban blocks, accommodating over eleven thousand of the dead of the rural battlefields. Even rough-hewn German bunkers were absorbed by the city's irenic expansion.

Rain has cratered and pocked the earth around the head-stones, smeared them with mud. The grass has been worn bare in places. The sky is grey with cold. Flowers have been pruned back to their stems. It is easy to imagine that the shedding of leaves is only the first stage in nature's cutting back for winter. In time branches will shrink back into trunks and trunks into earth until only frost-ravaged headstones remain above the ground.

It is so cold that we stay only a short time before Paul says,

'Let's get back in the car.'

'Tank, Paul, tank.'

'Sorry. "Tank." '

'And say "sir" when you say "tank".'

'Tank, sir. Yes, sir.'

Our next stop is the Hill 60 Museum, which for the rest of the trip we refer to as the Little Shop of Horrors. If Hill 60 seemed out of place in that list of sinister names – a stray from Vietnam – this place soon persuades you of its right to be included among them. Out front is a 'theme' café decorated with wartime bric-à-brac. One of those creepy old war songs is playing on a scratchy gramophone: 'It's a long way to Tipperary ...' The canned past.

The first room of the museum proper is given over mainly to stereoscopic viewers. Bright sepia in 3-D: lines of blasted trees receding into history; an exaggerated perspective on the past. Everything is covered in dust, 'the flesh of time' Brodsky calls it, 'time's very flesh and blood'. The walls are lined with photo-graphs, photographs of the muddy dead. Another trench song, 'The Old Battalion', scratches and crackles through the speakers:

If you want to find the old battalion,
I know where they are:
They're hanging on the old barbed wire.
I've seen 'em, I've seen 'em,
Hanging on the old barbed wire.

The next room is given over to hideous uniforms and a random assortment of broken bayonets, revolvers and shell casings. There are a couple of petrified boots, the remains of a rifle so rusty it looks like it has been salvaged from a coral reef. A dusty damp smell – damp rot, rotting dust – pervades the place. It is as if Steptoe and Son have opened up their own branch of the Imperial War Museum.

Through a glass door we step out into the rain-clogged trenches and ditches. Everything here is rusty. Not just the strips of corrugated iron which, let's face it, were designed to rust, but the earth and leaves. The year is turning to rust. Mud is old rust with dirt mixed in. Water is liquid rust.

By now the tank is a slum. It is littered with pâté rind, bread crumbs, greaseproof paper, orange peel and banana skins. Tins of beer rattle across the floor every time we turn a corner. From the outside hardly a square inch of the original paintwork can be seen. Even the interior is caked with mud from our boots.

Paul is driving. We are waiting at a junction. He begins pulling out on to the main road.

'Watch out!'

A truck, overtaking a car on the main road, thunders past, missing us by inches. We're all stunned. We talk about nothing else for the next hour.

'Think of the publicity that would have got for your book,' says Mark. 'Getting killed before you even wrote it.'

'This is not a book about Paul's driving,' I say. 'English poetry is not yet fit to speak of it.'

'Dulce et decorum est in tankus mori,' says Paul.

Messines Ridge Cemetery is set back from the road, in the middle of a quiet wood. The graves are strewn with leaves: yellow, flecked with black, brown-green. At the back of the cemetery is an arcade of classical pillars. Even the slightest breeze is enough to tug leaves from the trees. The rustle of a pheasant breaking free of the silence. Rain dripping through trees. Damp bird calls.

The headstones are turning green with moss. The words 'Their Glory Shall Not Be Blotted Out' are blotted out by mud splashed up by rain.

As each year passes, it grows more difficult to keep time at bay. A quarter of a century's moss forms in one year. Time is trying to make up for lost time. Left untended this cemetery, with its classical pillars, would look like an ancient ruin in a couple of years. If the machine-gun's unprecedented destructive power made it 'concentrated essence of infantry', then here we have concentrated essence of the past. This is the look the past tends towards.

We come to the vast German cemetery at Langemark. A pile of horse dung lies, accidentally, I suppose, in the entrance. Nearly 25,000 men are buried here in a mass grave. At the edge of the *Kameradengrab* stand four mourning figures, silhouetted against the zinc sky. Up close these are poorly sculpted figures, but from a distance they impart a sense of utter desolation to the place. It is as if the minute's silence for which they have bowed their heads has been extended for the duration of eternity. Names are printed on low grey pillars. To the right there are individual graves marked by flat slabs of stone.

There is no colour here, no flowers, nothing transcendent. The dead as individuals hardly matter; only as elements of the nation. There are no individual inscriptions, no rhetoric. Only the unadorned facts of mortality – and even these are reduced to a bare, bleak minimum. This is the meaning and consequence of defeat.

The French cemetery at Notre Dame de Lorette covers twenty-six acres. There are 20,000 named graves here; in the ossuary lie the remains of another 20,000 unknown dead. It is icy cold. Wind streams across the grey hill. Wind is not something that passes through the sky. The sky is wind and nothing else. Crosses stretch away in lines so long they seem to follow the curvature of the earth. Names are written on both the front and back of each cross. The scale of the cemetery exceeds all imagining. Even the names on the crosses count for nothing. Only the numbers count, the scale of loss. But this is so huge that it is consumed by itself. It shocks, stuns, numbs. Sassoon's nameless names here become the numberless numbers. You stand aghast while the wind hurtles through your clothes, searing your ears until you find yourself almost vanishing: in the face of this wind, in this expanse of lifelessness, you cannot hold your own: you do not count. There is no room here for the living. The wind, the cold, force you away.

We head south, following the Western Front down towards the Somme. We entertain ourselves by singing 'The Old Battalion' or conversing in a pseudo Great War lingo. Paul and I address Mark as Private Hayhurst and prefix everything with an officerly 'I say' or 'Look here'. For his part Mark, while adopting the tones of the loyal batman, is actually a scrimshanker who does nothing except sit in the back reading *Death's Men*. Our hotel is a 'billet'. The forthcoming night in the boozer is referred to as 'the show' or 'stunt'. None of us is quite sure whether we're on a gloomy holiday or a rowdy pilgrimage.

We are not the first to be uncertain on this score. During the twenties the British Legion and the St Barnabas Society organized subsidized trips to enable relatives of the dead who could not afford the journey to make a pilgrimage to the cemeteries where their loved ones lay.

Helen Turrell makes such a pilgrimage in Kipling's haunting, lovely story 'The Gardener'. Helen has brought up her nephew Michael ever since his father – her brother – died in India. Michael is killed in the war and buried in Hagenzeele Third Military Cemetery. It is a huge cemetery and only a few hundred of the twenty thousand graves are yet marked by white head-stones; the rest are marked by 'a merciless sea of black crosses'. Overwhelmed by the wilderness of graves, Helen approaches a man who is kneeling behind a row of headstones. 'Evidently a gardener', the man asks who she is looking for and Helen gives her nephew's name.

The man lifted his eyes and looked at her with infinite compassion before he turned from the fresh-sown grass towards the naked black crosses.

'Come with me,' he said, 'and I will show you where your son lies.'

The story all but ends there, with the words of this Christlike figure. A three-line epilogue records that when Helen left the cemetery she looked back and saw the man bending over his plants once again, 'supposing him to be the gardener'.

Like Helen, most of the pilgrims were bereaved women, but their numbers soon came to include veterans wanting to revisit the battlefields. Comforts were few on such trips, but there were also large numbers of visitors who wanted – and were willing to pay for – a less arduous and sombre trip around the trenches and cemeteries of France and Flanders: tourists, in short. In another instance of historical projection these battlefield tours had already been bitterly satirized by Philip Johnstone in his poem 'High Wood', first published in February 1918:

> Madame, please,
> You are requested kindly not to touch
> Or take away the Company's property
> As souvenirs; you'll find we have on sale
> A large variety, all guaranteed.

As I was saying, all is as it was,
This is an unknown British officer,
The tunic having lately rotted off.
Please follow me – this way...
      the *path*, sir, *please*...

Lyn Macdonald is perhaps exaggerating when she describes Ypres in 1920 as 'the booming mecca of the first mass-explosion of tourism in history', but in 1930 a hundred thousand people signed the visitors' book at the Menin Gate in just three months. Many came in the spirit of Johnstone's visitors or Abe North, who, in the Newfoundland Memorial Park, showers Dick Diver and Rosemary in a mock grenade attack of 'earth gobs and pebbles'; many more departed in the spirit of Dick himself who 'picked up a retaliatory handful of stones and then put them down.

' "I couldn't kid here," he said rather apologetically.'

Understandably as well as apologetically, for few novels are as saturated with the memory of the Great War as *Tender is the Night*. Dick himself sums up this central concern of the book with the 'half-ironic phrase, "Non-Combatant's shell-shock"'.

On the first page, as Dick makes his way to Zurich in 1917, he passes 'long trains of blinded or one-legged men, or dying trunks'. The clinic where he first meets Nicole is 'a refuge for the broken, the incomplete, the menacing'. Nicole's mental instability may not be related to the war – 'the war is over', she says, 'and I scarcely knew there was a war' – but is all the time reminding us of it. Her smile 'was like all the lost youth in the world'. Lost youth may be a perpetual theme of Fitzgerald's but there is often a larger historical dimension to our most personal concerns. In 1947, seven years after her husband's death, Zelda wrote in a letter: 'I do not know that a personality can be divorced from the times which evoke it ... I feel that Scott's greatest contribution was the dramatization of a heart-broken + despairing era ...' In 1917 Fitzgerald himself wrote: 'After all, life hasn't much to offer except youth and ... Every man I've met who's been to war, that is this war, seems to have lost youth and faith in man.'

All around Nicole at the clinic, meanwhile, are those maimed mentally or vicariously by the war: 'shell-shocks who merely heard an air raid from a distance' or 'merely read newspapers'. The accessories of fashion – a beret, for example – seek to cover 'a skull recently operated on. Beneath it human eyes peered.' Despite Nicole's immense wealth, even the idyllic period of their courtship is surrounded ominously by the sound of war:

Suddenly there was a booming from the wine slopes across the lake; cannons were shooting at hail-bearing clouds in order to break them ... the hotel crouched amid tumult, chaos, and darkness.

Years later, by which time his marriage to Nicole is showing signs of strain and he is falling for another, younger woman, Dick and his friends make their tour of the Newfoundland trenches.

We arrive there on a November morning. The sky is armistice-white. The trenches are still preserved but without the barbed wire – removed, finally, because sheep kept getting tangled up in it – the grass-covered shell-holes make the place look like a particularly difficult golf course.

Fitzgerald, by contrast, deliberately begins the section of the novel which describes Dick's visit, 'Casualties', so as to make it seem, for a moment, either as if the scene is taking place in the middle of the actual war or – and it amounts to the same thing – as if the war is still being waged in 1925:

Dick turned the corner of the traverse and continued along the trench walking on the duckboard. He came to a periscope, looked through it a moment, then he got up on the step and peered over the parapet. In front of him beneath a dingy sky was Beaumont-Hamel; to his left the tragic hill of Thiepval.

A few minutes later, by which time it has become clear that

the friends are simply visitors rather than combatants – though they are, of course, 'casualties' – Fitzgerald vouchsafes to Dick one of the most famous, beautiful and telling of all passages about the war.

See that little stream – we could walk to it in two minutes. It took the British a month to walk to it – a whole empire walking very slowly, dying in front and pushing forward behind. And another empire walked very slowly backward a few inches a day, leaving the dead like a million bloody rugs. No European will ever do that again in this generation . . .

This western-front business couldn't be done again, not for a long time. The young men think they could do it but they couldn't. They could fight the first Marne again but not this. This took religion and years of plenty and tremendous sureties and the exact relation between the classes.

Despite the cold there were a handful of other visitors at the Memorial Park. The smaller cemeteries are deserted. Sometimes there are intervals of three or four weeks in the visitors' books. Often people come to visit one particular grave: a great uncle, a grandfather. They are always touching, these personal inscriptions in the book, especially when the pilgrimage is the fulfilment of a lifetime's ambition.

Most comments, though, are generic: 'RIP', 'Remembering', 'We Will Remember Them', 'Lest We Forget', 'Very Moving'. Sometimes there is a jaunty salute: 'All the best, lads', 'Sleep well, boys'. As well as commenting on the cemetery itself – 'Peaceful', 'Beautiful' – many people offer larger impressions of the war: 'Such a waste', 'No more war', 'Never again'. All comments are heartfelt, even those like 'They died for freedom' or 'For Civilization', which, testifying to the enduring power of ignorance, end up meaning the opposite of what is intended: 'They died for nothing.' At the Connaught Cemetery for the massacred Ulster Division several visitors from Northern Ireland have written 'No surrender'. One entry, from Andy Keery, reads: 'No surrender. Proud to come from Ulster.' Beneath it his friend has written 'No surrender. I came with Andy.' Occasionally people quote a couple of lines of poetry. I add my own little couplet:

> A lot of people have written 'no surrender'.
> That's how bigots remember.

Sometimes people's comments are so idiosyncratic as scarcely to make sense: 'The bloke on the tractor spoiled it for me by his reckless driving. Signed anon' – the unknown visitor. On 10 October 1992 at Tyne Cot Greg Dawson wrote, 'We really showed those fascists a thing or two!' Another person had drawn a Star of David and written, 'What about the 6 million Jews?' Beneath it someone else had written, 'Wrong war, mate.' This quickly becomes something of a catch phrase between the three of us: irrespective of its relevance, any remark elicits the droll rejoinder, 'Wrong war, mate.'

At the Sheffield Memorial a diligent student wrote a short essay pointing out, in closely reasoned detail, that blame for the Somme rested, ultimately, on Churchill's shoulders. He even added a footnote citing A. J. P. Taylor, complete with page reference, place and date of publication. Reluctant to get drawn into the minutiae of scholarly debate, another visitor had simply scrawled in the margin: 'Rubbish!'

Sometimes a dialogue does evolve, most obviously at one of the Redan Ridge cemeteries. The theme of the discussion here is exactly that announced by the anti-Taylorite at the Sheffield Memorial: rubbish.

There are three tiny, beautifully located cemeteries at Redan Ridge. Next to one of them is a stinking mound of farm rubbish. An entry from 10 July 1986 expresses the characteristic sentiments of most visitors: 'It's such a shame they must rest with a rubbish pit beside them.'* Several pages on, after numerous endorse-

---

* The rubbish-tip controversy has obvious echoes with the fuss in 1981 over the then Labour leader Michael Foot turning up for the Remembrance Day Service at the Cenotaph wearing a donkey jacket. According to the *Daily*

ments of these remarks, the first dissenting voice appears: 'If visitors fail to recognize the true pathos behind their visits here only to latch on to the presence of a rubbish dump, then *their* presence here disgusts me.'

This attempt to scotch the debate only inflames it. The characteristic tone becomes aggressively indignant: 'The rubbish is a thinly disguised insult to the memory of Pte. Tommy Atkins.' Adding injury to insult the next person to join in notes: 'It's quite apt: human waste next to more of it.' Comments like this mean that from now on the ire of those offended by the rubbish is directed not only against the farmer who dumped it but against those who implicitly condone him – and who, in turn, become steadily more aggressive in their responses: 'Sod the rubbish-tip – these men lived and died in it. Isn't rubbish a part of life?'

That's a moot point, but for quite a few months now the rubbish has been playing a more important part in the visitors' book than the cemetery. Gradually the debate itself becomes the main subject of debate. The cemetery was ousted by the rubbish-tip; now both are only incidental to the real focus of attention: the visitors' book itself. You can imagine it being integrated into battlefield tours, becoming the main reason for people's visit. Conscious of this, someone has written: 'Quite frankly the wastage of human life is worthy of more comment than a ridiculous rubbish-tip saga.'

Every attempt to have the last word, however, demands a response and so the rubbish debate and the debate about the rubbish debate perpetuate themselves. It comes as something of a disappointment to read, on 9 September 1991: 'Glad the rubbish has finally gone.'

I note all this down on 9 November 1992. It is the second time I have been here and there is a strange pleasure in standing in

---

Telegraph, Foot laid his wreath 'with all the reverent dignity of a tramp bending down to inspect a cigarette end'.

exactly the same spot again. I find the proof of my last visit, in my own handwriting, in the visitors' book. It was a different season then; now the sky sags like mud over the brown earth. The air is cold as iron. Rain is blowing horizontal. The smell of rotting farmyard waste pervades the scene. I write:

> Returned here after my previous visit 5.9.91.
> PS: The rubbish has returned too.

The pages of these visitors' books are clipped in a green ring-hooped binder. When there are no pages left, new ones are clipped in. What happens to the old ones? Burned? Filed away in archives? If the latter, then perhaps an academic will one day salvage all these pages and use this hoard of raw data as the basis of a comprehensive survey of attitudes to the war, the ways in which it is remembered and misremembered. There is certainly enough material to fill a book: people who come here are moved and want to record their feelings, explain themselves.

And *this* book, really, is just an extended entry, jotted on pages ripped from the visitors' book of a cemetery on the Somme.

What with the weather and the escalating cost of the trip, we decide to abandon our plan to be at Thiepval for Armistice Day. I am all for continuing with the big push to Ors, where Owen is buried, but by now serious questions are being raised about my leadership. Paul and Mark are refusing to budge.

'You'll damn well go where I order you,' I say at last.

'What are you going to do? Court-martial us?' says Mark.

'Yeah. Fuck off, Hitler,' says Paul.

'Wrong war, mate,' chant Mark and I.

We decide to head back to Vimy Ridge (missed on the way down due to a navigational error) before beating a retreat to Boulogne.

Since Armistice Day has been incorporated into Remembrance Day, there is little point remaining here until the eleventh, but, as we drive towards Vimy, I ponder the significance of dates – 4 August 1914, 1 July 1916, 11 November 1918 – and the extent to which the ebbing and flowing of the memory of the Great War are determined by the gravitational pull of the calendar.

In his study of Holocaust memorials, James Young points out how

when events are commemoratively linked to a day on the calendar, a day whose figure inevitably recurs, both memory of events and the meanings engendered in memory seem ordained by nothing less than time itself.

The actual date of the event to be commemorated often falls as arbitrarily as a person's birthday. In the case of the Great War, which ended punctually at the eleventh hour of the eleventh day of the eleventh month, the temporal significance of the moment and day on which hostilities ceased was consciously predetermined. If the intention was to bring the future memory of the war into the sharpest possible focus, it could hardly have been better arranged: the various ceremonies of Remembrance could not have worked so powerfully without this precise temporal anchoring. Since the Second World War, this anchoring has been lost. Remembrance Day can now drift three days clear of the eleventh of November. Hence the sense noted earlier that at the Cenotaph it is the act of remembering together that is being remembered. Past and present are only imperfectly aligned.

In other ways they are being pulled into closer proximity. This was felt especially strongly in 1993, the centenary of Owen's birth and the seventy-fifth anniversary of his death: another example of the way in which the war has become memorialized in the poet's image. The same year also saw the seventy-fifth anniversary of the armistice. 4 August 1994 marked the eightieth anniversary of the outbreak of war. All of these dates are signposts pointing to one of the ways in which the memory of the Great War exerts itself more powerfully as it recedes in time. This has less to do with recent events in Sarajevo than the simple sense that we are drawing gradually closer to the time when the war took place exactly a hundred years ago. In terms of remembrance the years 2014–2018 will represent the temporal equivalent of a total eclipse. By then no one who fought in the war will be alive to remember it.

> 'The thousands of marriages
> Lasting a little while longer . . .'

Like the Newfoundland Memorial, the other major Canadian memorial, at Vimy Ridge, is located in an expanse of parkland in which the original trenches have been neatly maintained. A road winds up to the park through thick woods. Then, suddenly, the monument looms into view: two white pylons, each with a sculpted figure perched precariously near the top. Sunlight knifes through the clouds.

Twin white paths stretch across the grass. The steps to the monument are flanked by two figures, a naked man and a naked woman. The stone is dazzling white. It is difficult to estimate the height of the pylons. A hundred feet? Two hundred? Imposs- ible to say: there is nothing around to stand comparison with the monument. It generates its own scale, dwarfing the idea of measurement. At its base, between the two pylons, is a group of figures thrusting a torch upwards towards the figures perched high above. The distance between them is measureless.

Carved on the walls are the names of Canada's missing: 11,285 men with no known graves. I walk round to the east side of the monument where a group of figures are breaking a sword. Far off, in the other corner, is another similar group whose details I cannot make out at this distance. Between them, brooding over a vast sea of grass, is the shrouded form of a woman, her stone robes flowing over the ground. The figure spans millennia of grieving women, from pietàs showing the weeping Virgin to photos of widowed peasant women wrapped in shawls against

Vimy Ridge: the Canadian war memorial

the cold. Below her, resting on a tomb, are a sword and steel
helmet, the shadows of the twin pylons stretching out across the
grass.

The Memorial took eleven years to construct. Unveiled,
finally, in 1936, it was the last of the great war memorials to be
completed. Walter Allward, the sculptor and designer, explained
its symbolism in the following terms. The grieving woman
represents Canada, a young nation mourning her dead; the
figures to her left show the sympathy of Canada for the helpless;
to her right the Defenders are breaking the sword of war.
Between the pillars, Sacrifice throws the torch to his comrades;
high up on the pylons are allegorical figures of Honour, Faith,
Justice, Hope, Peace ... This string of virtues recalls a speech

Grief . . .

made by Lloyd George in September 1914 in which he itemized

the great everlasting things that matter for a nation – the great peaks
we had forgotten, of Honour, Duty, Patriotism and, clad in glittering
white, the great pinnacle of Sacrifice pointing like a rugged finger to
Heaven.

In its glittering whiteness Allward's monument seems the
shorn embodiment of Lloyd George's words. Duty and Patriotism have fallen away; Honour takes its place alongside Hope
and peace as allegorical decoration; Sacrifice remains undiminished: unmeasurable, sheer – but its meaning, too, has been
transformed by the war. It is here confronted with the consequence of its meaning.

Discounting the allegorical 'Defenders' there are no military figures on the monument. The steel helmet on the tomb is the only clear symbolic link with the war it commemorates. The figures at the base of the pylons strain upward, straining to rise above their grief, to surmount it until, like the figures nestling in the sky above them, they can overcome it. This vertiginous transcendence is counterpoised by the earthward gaze of the woman. Mute with sorrow she makes no appeal to the heavens but fixes her eyes on the ground, making an accommodation with grief, residing in loss.

Owen, wrote C. Day Lewis, 'had no pity to spare for the suffering of bereaved women'. Vimy Ridge, by contrast, seems less a memorial to the dead, to the abstract ideal of Sacrifice, than to the reality of grief: a memorial not to the Unknown Soldier but to Unknown Mothers.

I remember reading of a soldier's visit to the mother of a dead friend: ' "I've lost my only boy," was all she said, then became mute with grief.'

And then, as sometimes happens, this word 'grief' that I have used many times floats free of meaning and becomes a sound, an abstract arrangement of letters whose sense is suddenly lost. Grief, grief, grief. I say the word to myself until, gradually, it is reunited with the meaning it has always had.

I was living in New Orleans when the Gulf War ended. The city was swathed in yellow ribbons and each night I watched news reports about soldiers returning home to their loved ones, their sweethearts. Hugs and tears, brass bands playing, kisses, babies born while their fathers were away in the desert of Kuwait.

But what about the soldier with no girlfriend, no wife, no sweetheart to return to? The loner. Returning to nothing, surrounded by tickertape reunions, reminding me of a photograph from the Great War there was no one around to take.

Sepia weather. Shouldering his kit, making for the railway station. Heading home through force of habit. Holding his peace, coughing. The sky sagging over damp shires. The names of stations. Dead men's faces. Rain falling on smoke-stained towns. From now on this is what life will be: staring through a rain-grimed window, waiting for the journey to be over with. Houses and brooks passing by. Fields of wet nettles.

From the car, glancing back, the sculptures clinging to the sides of the two pylons give them the look of war-ravaged trees: blasted white trunks from which the stumps of branches protrude.

'The charred skeletons of the trees'

Barbusse's terse entry in his *War Diary* is echoed, repeated or expanded upon in almost every account of the war. Harold Macmillan thought 'the most extraordinary thing about the modern battlefield is the desolation and emptiness of it all. Nothing is to be seen of war or soldiers – only the split and shattered trees.' Writing to Ezra Pound in June 1917, Wyndham Lewis noted that 'shells never seem to do more than shave the trees down to these ultimate black stakes...'

Trees were not the only things to display the resilience of the vertical. There were remains of buildings like 'the famous Cloth Hall looking stark and naked with one wall standing' in the centre of Ypres. Or there were the ubiquitous calvaries ('One ever hangs where shelled roads part'), the most famous of which, again in Ypres, in the cemetery, remained miraculously intact after a dud shell lodged between the cross and the figure of the suffering Christ. As often as not these roadside crucifixes were sinister and troubling reminders of mortality rather than images of redemption. Having endured a long, terrifying wait on 'Mount Calvary' – the Germans can all the time be heard mining beneath them – the squad in Raymond Dorgeles' *Wooden Crosses* is finally relieved. As they march quickly away, leaving other men to take their place on the powder keg, Dorgeles looks back: 'The Calvary

'Totenlandschaft'

stood out terrible, a dreadful thing against the green night, with its battered stumps of trees like the uprights of a cross.' A history of the Gloucesters recalls that

The cemetery at Richebourg was an eerie spot; it had been completely churned up by shell-fire: tombs torn open to reveal skeletons that had lain there for years. The crucifix, as was so often the case, remained standing.

With its shattered trees and 'eerie' calvaries this war-ravaged landscape felt, in Sassoon's words, 'like the edge of the world'. On wet days 'the trees a mile away were like ash-grey smoke rising from the naked ridges, and it felt very much as if we were at the end of the world'.

Fussell uses passages like these to show how English writers viewed the war through a filter of 'ritual and romance' – specifically, in Sassoon's case, William Morris's *The Well at the World's End*. Ironically, this world's end landscape in which the English poets found themselves was the realization in hideous, distorted form of the great visions of German Romanticism.

Freed from their immediate context, passages like these add

up to an evocation of landscape that had been set down on canvas over a century earlier by Caspar David Friedrich. His *Abbey Under Oak Trees* of 1810 shows ravaged trees and the remains of a church rising through the mist; a funerary procession of figures bears a coffin through graves scattered haphazardly across the

The ruins of Ypres Cathedral, summer 1916

foreground. The German poet Karl Theodor Korner referred to this picture in 1815 as a *Totenlandschaft*, 'a landscape of the dead'. Exactly a century later Robert Musil, serving as an officer in the Austrian army, used precisely the same word to describe the scene he had witnessed on the Italian front.

As the war took its toll, even archetypal Romantic remnants like the ruined walls of abbeys were frequently blasted beyond recognition. At the edge of the allied world, near Ypres, all that could be seen was 'a sea of mud. Literally a sea.' In 1917 Blunden looked out across 'a dead sea of mud' and Stephen Graham, revisiting the area in 1920, was confronted by a 'land-ocean'. When the film director D. W. Griffith travelled to the Western Front as part of his preparation for the film *Hearts of the World*, he was disappointed by the dramatic potential of the war:

As you look out over No Man's Land there is literally nothing that meets the eye but an aching desolation of nothingness ... No one can describe it. You might as well try to describe the ocean.

The wife of an artist friend of Friedrich's was similarly dis-

The Monk by the Sea, by Caspar David Friedrich

appointed by the 1809 painting *The Monk by the Sea*: there was nothing to look at. 'By any earlier standards,' notes art historian Robert Rosenblum,

she was right: the picture is daringly empty, devoid of objects ... devoid of everything but the lonely confrontation of a single figure, a Capuchin monk, with the hypnotic simplicity of a completely unbroken horizon line, and above it a no less primal and potentially infinite extension of gloomy, hazy sky.

With only a minimum of changes, Rosenblum's words can serve equally well as a description of a panoramic photograph by William Rider-Rider which reproduces Friedrich's vision in the devastated battlefield of Passchendaele.

The scene is divided evenly between land and sky. A line of blasted trees separates the shattered foreground from the land-ocean, the sea of mud, which, as in *The Monk by the Sea*, reaches to the horizon. Instead of receding into the distance, these trees disappear beyond the edges of the frame. There is no perspective. The vanishing-point is no longer a more or less exact point, but all around. A new kind of infinity: more of the same in every direction, an infinity of waste. The sky lies in tatters in the mud.

An infinity of waste

It is impossible to tell what time of day the photo was taken. There is no direct source of light – just the grey luminosity of the sky. In the middle of the picture, instead of Friedrich's monk, there is an unknown soldier, smoking. Nothing is moving. Hence, despite the endless desolation, the strange serenity of the photograph.

Ruins, for the Romantics, fulfilled the useful function of being enduring monuments to transience: what faded as grandeur survived as ruins. As testaments to their own survival, ruins, typically, had the story of their own ruination inscribed within them. Wordsworth established an imaginative template with the stories of silent suffering read in the ruins of 'Michael' or 'The Ruined Cottage'. So pervasive was the cult of ruination that a ruin became a place where a certain set of responses lay perfectly intact.

The Great War ruined the idea of ruins. Instead of the slow patient work of ruination observed in Shelley's 'Ozymandias', artillery brought about instant obliteration. Things survived only be accident or chance – like the calvary at Ypres – or mistake. Destruction was the standard and the norm. Cottages and villages did not crumble and decay – they were swept away.

In France, researching his book on the Battle of the Somme in March 1917, John Masefield described the area around Serre as

skinned, gouged, flayed and slaughtered, and the villages smashed to powder, so that no man could ever say there had been a village there within the memory of man.

In Barbusse's *Under Fire* the squad are making their way to the village of Souchez when the narrator realizes they are already there:

In point of fact we have not left the plain, the vast plain, seared and barren – but we are in Souchez!

The village has disappeared ... There is not even an end of wall, fence, or porch that remains standing.

Revisiting the scenes of battle near Passchendaele in 1920, Stephen Graham finds himself – or loses himself, more accurately – in what Barbusse calls a 'plain of lost landmarks':

The old church of Zandwoorde cannot now be identified by any ruins – one has to ask where it was. Even the bricks and the stones seem to have been swept away.

Considering the same area of land half a century later, Leon Wolff puts the scale of destruction in its historical context: 'In a later war, atomic bombs wrecked two Japanese cities; but Passchendaele was effaced from the earth.'

Shunning such emotive turns of phrase, Denis Winter emphasizes that the Somme presented a scene of devastation even more thorough than that observed in Belgium: 'Aerial photos of

Passchendaele in its final stages show grass and even trees. By autumn 1916, on the other hand, there was no vestige of grass on the Somme.'

Passchendaele, Albert and other villages in the Somme were rebuilt, but to some of the villages around Verdun the inhabitants never returned. Fleury, Douaumont and Cumières vanished from the map for ever.

Ruins rise from the ashes of the Great War with the Nazis and Albert Speer's 'Theory of Ruin Value'. Instead of being remnants of the past, Speer's ruins are projected into a distant future – a future stretching even beyond the thousand-year Reich. With Hitler's enthusiastic approval Speer set about designing structures and using materials to ensure that, even after generations of decay, the ivy-grown columns and crumbling walls of the Reich would have the ruined splendour of the great models of antiquity.

In the occupied countries the all–obliterating destruction of the Great War could be raised by the Nazis to the level of strategic principle. The fate of the Czech village of Lidice has been described by Albert Camus. The houses were burned to the ground, the men were shot, the women and children deported. After that

special teams spent months at work levelling the terrain with dynamite, destroying the very stones, filling in the village pond and, finally, diverting the course of the river ... To make assurance doubly sure, the cemetery was emptied of its dead who might have been a perpetual reminder that once something existed in this place.

The passion for Remembrance – for building memorials, for recording the names of the dead – can be better understood in the wake of such destruction. Solace and comfort can be found in the capacity of ruins to survive the human tragedies they result from and record. But the destruction first witnessed in the Great War was so thorough that it seemed capable of obliterating all trace of itself. Men were blown to pieces or disappeared into mud, villages were lost without trace. All that would remain, it seemed, would be 'a sponge, an infernal swamp for souls in pain'.

Soldiers returned from this zone of obliteration to an England virtually untouched by war. The Second World War left London and other major cities cratered and ravaged by the Blitz. After the Great War the architecture and landscape of England were unchanged except, here and there, for relatively slight damage from air raids. Apart from the injured, there was no sign of a war having taken place. Written in October 1918, Cynthia Asquith's words were prescient:

I am beginning to rub my eyes at the prospect of peace. I think it will require more courage than anything that has gone before ... one will at last fully recognize that the dead are not only dead for the duration of the war.

It was as if a terrible plague had swept invisibly through the male population of the country – except there were no bodies, no signs of burial, no cemeteries even. Ten per cent of the males under forty-five had simply disappeared.

Life went on. 'We didn't really miss the men who didn't come back,' a native of Akenfield remarks. 'The village stayed the same.' An accurate analysis, it turns out, of the demographic consequences of the war; in the 1921 national census the age distribution curve compared with 1901 and 1966 'reveals hardly the slightest difference'. In the cold light of population statistics, in other words, the losses of the terrible battles were soon made good.

The problem, then, was to find a way of making manifest the memory of those who were missing – who did not *figure* in statistics like these. How to make visible this invisible loss? How to do the work of ruins? How to inscribe the story of what had happened on a death-haunted landscape which was, apparently, unmarked by the greatest tragedy to have affected the nation? Again we come back to Owen's 'Anthem', which, by cataloguing the ways in which the dead will not be remembered – 'no prayers nor bells' – etches their memory in the dusk of the shires.

In a fragment omitted from the published version of *Minima Moralia* Adorno observed that 'what the Nazis did to the Jews was unspeakable: language had no word for it'. And yet, 'a term needed to be found if the victims . . . were to be spared the curse of having no thoughts turned unto them. So in English the concept of genocide was coined.' As a result, Adorno continues, 'the unspeakable was made, for the sake of protest, commensurable'.

What happened in the Great War remained incommensurable. 'Horror' and 'slaughter' have become popular terms of shorthand response; at a higher level of emotional and verbal refinement there is Owen's 'pity'. Successive waves of rhetorical elaboration could never contain the experience in which they originated – this, paradoxically, is what gives the poetry its *appeal*: the cry of the poems is unanswerable. This is what was heard in the two minutes' silence of Armistice Day and is heard still in the perpetual silence of the cemeteries. Remembrance is the means by which the incommensurability of the Great War is acknowledged and expressed.

Parts of the Western Front, like the area of the Somme, had been so completely devastated that the French government contemplated making them into national forests. Soon after the armistice, however, peasants began drifting back to their old farms where they were granted three years' rent-free tenancy. Battlefields were levelled and cleared of war debris and dead; houses were rebuilt. Stephen Graham's *The Challenge of the Dead* offers an eyewitness account of the early stages of the Western Front's transition from war to peace. Again and again in the course of his travels he comes across parties of soldiers exhuming bodies from the earth. Amidst this harvest of death the first signs of returning life serve only to transform a featureless quagmire to a blighted wilderness, a landscape at once pre- and post-historic:

... trees not quite dead but sprouting green from black trunks and then to blasted trees dead to the core. After a mile or so farmhouses and cultivation cease and one enters the terrible battle area of Passchendaele, all pits, all tangled with corroded wire – but now as if it were in tumultuous conflict with Nature ... The stagnancy has not dried up, but festers still in black rot below the rushes. Double shell-holes, treble shell-holes, charred ground, great pits, bashed-in dug-outs, all overgrown with the highest of wild flowers...

In 1917 Masefield wrote letter after letter to his wife, cataloguing the devastation he was witnessing in the area of the Somme. Even while surrounded by destruction on an unimaginable scale, he predicted that 'when the trenches are filled in, when the plough has gone over them, the ground will not long keep the look of war'. By the late twenties he was being proved right. When R. H. Mottram went back twenty years after the end of the war, he found 'all semblance gone, irretrievably gone'. If at first the fear had been that the area was beyond renovation, now veterans became worried that insufficient traces would remain of what had taken place. In 1930 Vera Brittain wrote:

Nature herself conspires with time to cheat our recollections; grass has grown over the shell-holes at Ypres, and the cultivated meadows of industrious peasants have replaced the hut-scarred fields of Etaples and Camiers where once I nursed the wounded in their great retreat of 1918.

Carl Sandburg's poem 'Grass' transforms this vast capacity for rejuvenation from a source of anxiety to one of comfort.

And pile them high at Ypres and Verdun.
Shovel them under and let me work.
Two years, ten years, and passengers ask the conductor:
What place is this?
Where are we now?

I am the grass.
Let me work.

Fields stretch away yellow and green under a perfect sky. I walk along a footpath to a small cemetery on the top of a low hill. At the edge of the path is a small pile of shells. Dense with rust, they look like relics of the Bronze or Iron Age, from a time before there were cities or books.

Even the grass cannot work hard enough to keep these traces of the past buried for good. 'A farmer on the Western Front cannot prune a tree without ruining his saw,' claims a character in Ondaatje's *The English Patient*, 'because of the amount of shrapnel shot into it during the [Great] War.' Each year's ploughing brings new bodies to the surface. Each year, writes David Constantine,

> the ground breaks out in an eczema of iron,
> Lead and the bones of men and the poor horses . . .

The Missing of the Somme

Three p.m. The sun is blazing. The last mist melted hours ago. Trees gather the sky's blueness around themselves. The fields on either side of the road are blurred red by poppies. I take off my shirt and soon my rucksack is clammy with sweat. By this time on 1 July 1916, under a sky as clear and hot as this, 20,000 British soldiers had been killed; another 40,000 were wounded or missing.

As I make my way towards it, the memorial at Thiepval seems almost ugly, its hulking immensity dominating the landscape for miles around.

At the car park on the edge of the site a sign states that this memorial stands on sacred ground. Visitors are asked not to bring dogs here, not to picnic, to try to preserve the beauty and tranquillity of the place.

There is no one else here. A wind moves through the jade-green trees. Green and black seem shades of each other. The grass is clipped razor-short, blazing bright green as though its colour is intensified by being so confined: potential inches of colour crammed into a centimetre. I can imagine nowhere more beautiful.

On 28 April 1917, Masefield wrote a letter describing the scene he witnessed here:

Corpses, rats, old tins, old weapons, rifles, bombs, legs, boots, skulls, cartridges, bits of wood & tin & iron & stone, parts of rotting bodies & festering heads lie scattered about. A more filthy evil hole you cannot imagine.

At the edge of the grass there is a long curving stone seat, where I sit and watch the British and French flags breezing perfectly from the summit of the huge monument. For once even the Union Jack does not look ugly.

The sun burns on the letters high up on the memorial: THE MISSING OF THE SOMME.

By contrast to the missing it commemorates, the Thiepval Memorial is palpably here, unmissable.* Designed by Lutyens in High Empire style (if there is such a thing), there is no humility about it, no backing down, no regret.

Permanent, built to last, the monument has none of the vulnerability of the human body, none of its terrible propensity for harm. Its predominant relation is to the earth – not, as is the case with a cathedral, to the sky. A cathedral reaches up, defies gravity effortlessly, its effect is entirely vertiginous. And unlike a cathedral which is so graceful (full of grace) that, after a point, it disappears, becomes ethereal, the Thiepval Memorial, after a point, simply refuses to go any higher. It is stubborn,

---

* A monument to 'the untellable', it is also, strangely and appropriately, unphotographable. No photograph can convey its scale, its balance, its overwhelming effect on the senses.

stoical. Like the deadlocked armies of the war, it stands its ground.

The contrast with a cathedral is telling in another, broader sense. In keeping with Lutyens' general preference, the Memorial is stripped of Christian symbolism; there was, he felt, no need for it. For many men who survived, the Battle of the Somme (which, in memory, represents the core experience and expression of the Great War) put an end to the consoling power of religion. 'From that moment,' a soldier has said of the first day's fighting, 'all my religion died. All my teaching and beliefs in God had left me, never to return.' In some ways, then, the Thiepval Memorial is a memorial if not to the death, then certainly to the superfluousness of God. Commemorated here is the faith of the 'empty heaven' evoked in a moving passage by Manning:

These apparently rude and brutal natures comforted, encouraged, and reconciled each other to fate, with a tenderness and tact which was more moving than anything in life. They had nothing; not even their own bodies which had become mere implements of warfare. They turned from the wreckage and misery of life to an empty heaven, and from an empty heaven to the silence of their own hearts. They had been brought to the last extremity of hope, and yet they put their hands on each other's shoulders and said with a passionate conviction that it would be all right, though they had faith in nothing, but in themselves and in each other.

I cross the grass and walk up the shadow-mounted steps of the Memorial itself. A few wreaths have been left by the Great War Stone, their red petals glowing brightly against the pale stone. From here I can see that the monument is built on sixteen huge legs which come together in interlocking arches; also that it is made of brick. Concrete can be poured in a mass but bricks have to be placed individually just as, on each of the four sides of the sixteen legs, the names of the missing had to be carved on bands of white stone facing. (The design of the sixteen legs presumably originated in the need to create enough surface area to accommodate all the names in such a way – no more than five or six feet above head height – that they are easily readable.) Most names are here, arranged by regiments. Game W 27446, Game W 27448. There are several Dyers. High up, two plaques – French on one side, English on the other – explain that the names are recorded here of 73,077 men who lost their lives in the Battle of the Somme and to whom the fortunes of war denied the honour of proper burial.

I remember John Berger in a lecture suggesting that ours has been the century of departure, of migration, of exodus – of disappearance. 'The century of people helplessly seeing others, who were close to them, disappear over the horizon.' If this is so, then the Thiepval Memorial to the Missing casts a shadow into the future, a shadow which extends beyond the dead of the Holocaust, to the Gulag, to the 'disappeared' of South America and of Tiananmen.

There had been military disasters before the Battle of the Somme, but these – the Charge of the Light Brigade, for example – served only as indictments of individual strategy, not of the larger purpose of which they were a part. For the first time in history the Great War resulted in a sense of the utter waste and futility of war. If the twentieth century has drifted slowly towards an acute sense of waste as a moral and political issue, then the origins of the ecology of compassion (represented by the peace movement, most obviously) are to be found in the once-devastated landscape of the Somme.

That is why so much of the meaning of our century is concentrated here. Thiepval is not simply a site of commemoration but of prophecy, of birth as well as of death: a memorial to the future, to what the century had in store for those who were left, whom age would weary.

At the far side of the memorial there is a small cemetery. On the Cross of Sacrifice at the edge of the cemetery I read:

THAT THE WORLD MAY REMEMBER THE COMMON SACRIFICE
OF TWO AND A HALF MILLION DEAD HERE
HAVE BEEN LAID SIDE BY SIDE SOLDIERS OF FRANCE
AND OF THE BRITISH EMPIRE IN ETERNAL COMRADESHIP.

The cemetery is divided in two halves: French crosses on one
side, English headstones on the other. A place where time and
silence have stood their ground. In the distance, wheat fields and
low hedges, trees. I walk along rows of crosses on each of which
is written the single word: INCONNU. Row after row. On the
English side there are the pale headstones:

A SOLDIER
OF THE GREAT WAR
KNOWN UNTO GOD

In front of each grave there are flowers: flame-bursts of yellow,
pink, red, orange. Apart from roses I recognize none of the
flowers; the rest remain unknown, unnamed.

The only sound is of humming bees, of light passing through
trees, striking the grass. Gradually I become aware that the air is
alive with butterflies. The flowers are thick with the white blur
of wings, the rust and black camouflage of Red Admirals, silent
as ghosts. I remember the names of only a few butterflies but I
know that the Greek word *psyche* means both 'soul' and 'but-
terfly'. And as I sit and watch, I know also that what I am seeing
are the souls of the nameless dead who lie here, fluttering through
the perfect air.

It is early evening by the time I make my way to Beaumont-
Hamel. I walk along a footpath to a small cemetery on the top
of a low hill. From the cemetery gate I can see the crosses of
four other small cemeteries.

The headstones are arranged in three lines, facing east. It is a
perfect spot, without even the drone of cars to disturb it. The
light is softening, stretching out over the fields. Soft and sharp,

gentle and bright. I take out the register of graves. Cemetery Redan Ridge Number One: 154 soldiers lie here, 73 unidentified. As I look through the book, the sun makes the pages glow the same colour as the Great War Stone.

Few people come here: the first entry in the visitors' book was made in 1986, the last ten days ago. On 18 August 1988 a girl from the Netherlands had written: 'It is because of the lonelyness.'

Light, field, the crosses of the other cemeteries. The faint breeze makes the pages stir beneath my fingers. It is the opposite of lonely, this cemetery: friends are buried here together – so what truth do these strange words express? The harder I try to decipher them, the more puzzling they become until, recognizing how ingrained is my mistake, trying to break a code that is not even there, I let them stand for themselves, their mystery and power undisturbed, these words that explain everything and nothing.

Scarves of purple cloud are beginning to stretch out over the horizon, light welling up behind them. The sun is going down on one of the most beautiful places on earth.

I have never felt so peaceful. I would be happy never to leave.

So strong are these feelings that I wonder if there is not some compensatory quality in nature, some equilibrium – of which the poppy is a manifestation and symbol – which means that where terrible violence has taken place the earth will sometimes generate an equal and opposite sense of peace. In this place where men were slaughtered they came also to love each other, to realize Camus's great truth: that 'there are more things to admire in men than to despise'.

Standing here, I know that some part of me will always be calmed by the memory of this place, by the vast capacity for forgiveness revealed by these cemeteries, by this landscape.

At this moment I am the only person on earth experiencing these sensations, in this place. At the same time, overwhelming and compounding this feeling, is the certainty that my presence here changes nothing; everything would be exactly the same without me.

Perhaps that is what is meant by 'lonelyness' – knowing that even at your moments of most exalted emotion, you do not matter (perhaps this is precisely the moment of most exalted emotion) because these things will always be here: the dark trees full of summer leaf, the fading light that has not changed in seventy-five years, the peace that lies perpetually in wait.

The sky is streaked crimson by the time I leave the cemetery of Redan Ridge Number One. I make my way back towards the road through dark fields. Tomorrow, a year from now, it will be exactly the same: birds lunging and darting towards the horizon; three crosses silhouetted against the blood-red sky; a man walking along the curving road; lights coming on in distant farmhouses – and each slow dusk a drawing-down of blinds.

NOTES

Place of publication is London unless otherwise indicated. Full sources are given in the Notes only when the source is not obvious from the text or the Bibliography. Multi-part quotes may extend across more than one page, but the Notes reference is for the first part only.

p. 2   'On every mantelpiece ...': Yvan Goll, 'Requiem for the Dead of Europe', in Jon Silkin (ed.), *The Penguin Book of First World War Poetry*, p. 244.

p. 2   'Memory has a ...': John Updike, *Memories of the Ford Administration* (Hamish Hamilton, 1993) p. 9.

p. 3   'in his ghastly ...': Wilfred Owen, 'Disabled', *Collected Poems*, p. 67.

p. 5   'the turning-point in ...': *Men without Art*, extract reprinted in Julian Symons (ed.), *The Essential Wyndham Lewis*, p. 211.

p. 5   For an extended discussion of pre-1914 as a period of latent war see Daniel Pick, *War Machine* (1993), pp. 192–5.

p. 6   'breaking down even ...': A. J. P. Taylor, *Europe: Grandeur and Decline* (Penguin, Harmondsworth, 1991), p. 185.

p. 6   'maintain towards his ...': 'The Idea of History', in Fritz Stern (ed.), *The Varieties of History*, 2nd edn (Macmillan, 1970), p. 292.

p. 8   'prepared his exit ...' and 'We are setting ...': *Scott and Amundsen: The Race to the South Pole*, revised edn (Pan, 1983), p. 508.

p. 9   'has shown that ...': ibid., p. 523.

p. 9   'We are showing ...': ibid., p. 508.

p. 9   'Of their suffering ...': Thomas Williamson, quoted by Huntford, ibid., pp. 520–21.

p. 9   'if Scott fails ...': ibid., p. 394.

p. 9   'the grotesque futility ...': ibid., p. 527.

p. 9   'heroism for heroism's sake ...' and 'for one of ...': ibid., p. 523.

p. 10   'the glory of ...' and 'to make a ...': ibid., p. 524.

p. 10   'countrymen an example ...': Agnes Egerton-Castle, 'The Precursor', *The Treasure*, January 1916, pp. 71–2, quoted by Huntford, ibid., p. 528.

p. 10n 'a special effort ...' and 'An Exhibition of ...': Annual Report of the Church Crafts League, quoted by Catherine Moriarty, 'Christian Iconography and First World War Memorials', in the *Imperial War Museum Review*, no. 6, p. 67.

p. 10n 'to secure combined ...': Quoted by Bob Bushaway, 'Name upon Name: The Great War and Remembrance', in Roy Porter (ed.), *Myths of the English*, p. 144.

p. 11   'simplicity of statement ...': A. C. Benson, quoted by Bushaway, ibid., p. 146.

p. 12   'The graveyards, haphazard ...': Clayre Percy and Jane Ridley (eds.), *The Letters of Edwin Lutyens to his Wife Emily* (Collins, 1985), p. 350.

p. 12   For a history of the War Graves Commission see Philip Longworth, *The Unending Vigil*, Constable, 1967.

p. 14   'the image of ...': *Fallen Soldiers*, p. 39. For a fuller account of changing attitudes to death and cemetery design etc., see ibid., pp. 39–45.

p. 14   Statistics for burials in the Somme are from Martin and Mary Middlebrook, *The Somme Battlefields*, pp. 9–10.

p. 15   ' "The future!" ...': *Under Fire*, pp. 256–7.

p. 16n 'What kind of ...': quoted by Alistair Horne in *The Price of Glory: Verdun 1916*, p. 341.

p. 16   ' "It'll be ..." and 'sorrowfully, like a ...': pp. 327–8.

p. 17   'What passing-bells for ...': 'Anthem for Doomed Youth', *Collected Poems*, p. 44.

p. 17   ' "We *shall* forget ...": *Under Fire*, p. 328.

p. 17   'Remembering, we forget': 'To One Who was With Me in the War', *Collected Poems 1908–1956*, p. 187.

p. 17   'We're forgetting-machines ...': *Under Fire*, p. 328.

p. 18   'How the future ...': The Owen manuscript is reproduced by Dominic Hibberd in *Wilfred Owen: The Last Year*, p. 123.

p. 18   'no dividends from ...': *Collected Poems 1908–1956*, p. 71.

p. 18   'Have you forgotten ...', 'Look down, and ...' and 'Do you remember ...': ibid., pp. 118–19.

p. 19   'Make them forget': ibid., p. 201.

p. 19   'gather[ed] to itself ...': *The Challenge of the Dead*, p. 173.

p. 19   'some tribute to ...': quoted by David Cannadine, 'Death, Grief and Mourning in Modern Britain', in Joachim Whalley (ed.) *Mirrors of Mortality*, p. 220. I have also drawn on Cannadine's essay more generally in this section.

p. 19   'by the human ...': quoted by Cannadine, ibid., p. 221.

p. 20   'the great awful ...': *The Times*, 12 November 1919, p. 15.

p. 21   'the man who ...': Ronald Blythe, *The Age of Illusion*, new edn (Oxford University Press, Oxford, 1983), p. 9. Blythe's first chapter contains a detailed and evocative account of how the idea of burying an unknown soldier came about.

p. 21   'In silence, broken ...', et al.: Armistice Day Supplement, *The Times*, 12 November 1920, pp. i–iii.

p. 21n   'In the tarpaper ...': *USA* (Penguin, Harmondsworth, 1966), pp. 722–3. I am grateful to Nick Humphrey for putting me on to this passage.

p. 22   'All this was ...': quoted in David Cannadine, 'Death, Grief and Mourning in Modern Britain', in Joachim Whalley (ed.), *Mirrors of Mortality*, p. 224.

p. 22   Fabian Ware: quoted in Cannadine, ibid., p. 197.

p. 24   The draft of Owen's 'Apologia Pro Poemate Meo' is reproduced in Dominic Hibberd, *Wilfred Owen: The Last Year*, p. 74.

p. 24   'was a silence ...': 'The Untellable', *New Society*, 11 May 1978, p. 317.

p. 24   'the very pulse ...': Armistice Day Supplement, 12 November 1920, p. i.

p. 25   For fuller accounts of the evolution of the various rituals of Remembrance see the works listed in the Select Bibliography by Bob Bushaway, David Cannadine, George Mosse and Richard Garrett.

p. 25n   'treated as part ...': *Fallen Soldiers*, p. 49. For a thorough discussion of changing attitudes to the war dead see ibid., pp. 3–50.

p. 27   'Horrible beastliness of ...': from Owen's draft list of contents for his proposed book of poems, reproduced by Dominic Hibberd, *Wilfred Owen: The Last Year*, p. 123.

p. 28   'grimly appalling ...' and 'the very depths ...': *Images of Wartime*, p. 50.

p. 28   'The main purpose ...': *The Body in Pain*, p. 63. I am grateful to Valentine Cunningham for bringing this book to my attention.

p. 28   'before the Great ...': *The Old Lie*, p. 137.

p. 29   'begloried sonnets' and 'second-hand phrases': *Collected Works*, p. 237.

p. 29   'part of the ...': *The Art of Ted Hughes*, 2nd edn (Cambridge University Press, Cambridge, 1978), p. 30.

p. 31   'how great a ...': from Blunden's Memoir of Owen, reproduced in Wilfred Owen, *Collected Poems*, p. 147 (my italics).

p. 31   'even the men ...': 'My Country Right or Left', *The Collected Essays, Journalism and Letters,* vol. 1, pp. 589–90.

p. 31   'we young writers ...', et al.: *Lions and Shadows*, pp. 74–6.

p. 31   'became conscious of ...' and 'was that it ...': George Orwell, *The Collected Essays, Journalism and Letters*, vol. 1, pp. 589–90.

p. 31   'came home deepest ...': from introduction in Wilfred Owen, *Collected Poems*, p. 12.

p. 31   'easy acceptance of ...': Edward Mendelson (ed.), *The English Auden: Poems, Essays and Dramatic Writings 1927–1939* (Faber, 1977), p. 212.

p. 31   'the propagandist lie ...': quoted in Samuel Hynes, *The Auden Generation*, p. 249.

p. 32   'produced envy rather ...' and 'Even in our ...': *Friends Apart*, p. 91.

p. 33   'An Unveiling': *Collected Poems*, p. 204.

p. 33   'a real Cenotaph': quoted by Christopher Ridgeway in introduction to Richard Aldington, *Death of a Hero*.

p. 33   'a memorial in ...': *Death of a Hero*, p. 8.

p. 33   'What passing-bells for ...': *Collected Poems*, p. 44.

p. 34   'the official record ...' and 'vetted so as ...': *Haig's Command*, p. 4. For counter-charges concerning Winter's own manipulation of his material see John Hussey, 'The Case Against Haig:

Mr Denis Winter's Evidence', *Stand To: The Journal of the Western Front Association* (winter 1992), pp. 15–17.

p. 34 'passive suffering ...': from introduction to *Oxford Book of Modern Verse* (Oxford University Press, Oxford, 1936), p. xxxiv.

p. 35 'records of [Owen's] ...': facsimile edition reprinted by the Imperial War Museum 1990, p. v.

p. 35 'almost a spirit ...': 'The Real Wilfred', *Required Writing*, p. 230.

p. 35 'existed for some ...': ibid., p. 228.

p. 35 'the pall of...': David Cannadine, 'Death, Grief and Mourning in Modern Britain', in Joachim Whalley (ed.), *Mirrors of Mortality*, p. 233.

p. 35 For more on spiritualism in the 1920s see David Cannadine, ibid., pp. 227–31.

p. 35 'prophecies in reverse ...': *Camera Lucida* (Hill & Wang, New York, 1981), p. 87.

p. 35 'I began to ...': 'To Please a Shadow', *Less than One* (Penguin, Harmondsworth, 1987), p. 370.

p. 35n 'W. O. seems ...': letter to Robert Conquest, 9 January 1975, in Anthony Thwaite (ed.) *Selected Letters* (Faber, 1992), p. 519.

p. 36 'Grey monotony lending ...': P. J. Kavanagh (ed.), *Collected Poems*, p. 36.

p. 36 'I again work...': Felix Klee (ed.) *Diaries 1898–1918* (University of California Press, Berkeley, 1964), p. 380.

p. 36 'great sunk silences': Isaac Rosenberg, 'Dead Man's Dump', *Collected Works*, p. 111.

p. 36 'Those Harmsworth books ...': *Collected Poems* (Oxford University Press, Oxford, 1983), p. 40.

p. 36 'sepia November...': *New and Collected Poems* (Robson Books, 1980), p. 63.

p. 36 'in black and ...': *The Post-Modernist Always Rings Twice* (Fourth Estate, 1992), p. 79.

p. 36 'Having seen all ...': Wilfred Owen, 'Insensibility', *Collected Poems*, p. 37.

p. 37 'the choice of ...': 'Vlamertinghe: Passing the Château, July, 1917', *Undertones of War*, p. 256.

p. 37 'The year itself...': *The Wars*, p. 11.

p. 37   'long uneven lines . . .': *Collected Poems* (Faber, 1988), p. 128.

p. 37   'The Send-Off': *Collected Poems*, p. 46.

p. 38   'Agony stares from . . .': Edmund Blunden, 'The Zonnebeke Road', *Undertones of War*, p. 250.

p. 38   For a fuller account of restrictions on photographers see Jane Carmichael, *First World War Photographers*, pp. 11–21.

p. 39   'In the account . . .': the German Field Marshal was Paul Von Hindenberg, quoted in Peter Vansittart, *Voices from the Great War*, p. 145.

p. 39   'lay three or . . .': Peter Vansittart (ed.), *Letters from the Front* (Constable, 1984), p. 209.

p. 39   'Where do they . . .': quoted in Jon Glover and Jon Silkin (eds.), *The Penguin Book of First World War Prose*, p. 63.

p. 40   'of the very . . .' and 'an incomprehensible look . . .': *Collected Letters*, p. 521.

p. 40   Owen quoting Tagore: Jon Stallworthy, *Wilfred Owen*, p. 267.

p. 41   'As under a . . .': 'Dulce et Decorum Est', *Collected Poems*, p. 55.

p. 41   'indirectly by watching . . .': letter to Susan Owen, 4 (or 5) October 1918, *Collected Letters*, p. 580.

p. 41   'I saw their . . .': 'The Show', *Collected Poems*, p. 50.

p. 41   'O Love, your . . .': 'Greater Love' ibid., p. 41.

p. 41   ' "O sir, my . . .': 'The Sentry', ibid., p. 61.

p. 41   'If in some . . .': ibid., p. 55.

p. 41   'not concerned with . . .': 'Preface', *Collected Poems*, p. 31.

p. 42   'not interested in . . .': quoted in Richard Whelan, *Robert Capa: A Biography*, p. 176.

p. 42   'were swarming with . . .': ibid., p. 235.

p. 44   'Tenderness: something on . . .': from Henri Barbusse's *War Diary*, in Jon Glover and Jon Silkin (eds.), *The Penguin Book of First World War Prose*, p. 195.

p. 45   'I tell you . . .', 'could not cry . . .', et al.: Erich Maria Remarque, *All Quiet on the Western Front*, pp. 46–7.

p. 45n 'He spoke of . . .': (Picador, 1993), p. 111.

p. 45   'a herdsman', 'a Shepherd of . . .' and 'a cattle-driver': letters of 31 August and 1 September 1918, *Collected Letters*, pp. 570–71.

p. 45   'herded from the ...': 'The Sentry', *Collected Poems*, p. 61.

p. 46   'when the Other ...': *The Great War and Modern Memory*, p. 239.

p. 47   'happy in a ...': entry for 15 February 1917, *Diaries 1915–1918*, p. 132.

p. 47   'lives or affects ...': *Men without Art*, in Julian Symons (ed.), *The Essential Wyndham Lewis* p. 207 (italics in original).

p. 47   'The great wars ...': *Imagined Communities*, p. 131.

p. 47   'Being shelled ...': *Air with Armed Men* (London Magazine Editions 1972) p. 114.

p. 47   'One does not ...': quoted in Alistair Horne, *The Price of Glory: Verdun 1916*, p. 338.

p. 48   'The hero became ...': Modris Eksteins, *Rites of Spring*, p. 146.

p. 49   'personally manipulated a ...' and 'personally captured an ...': *Wilfred Owen: The Last Year*, p. 174.

p. 49   'had never seen ...': *Goodbye to All That*, p. 226.

p. 49   'incredibly pitiful wretches ...': *Under Fire*, p. 330.

p. 49   'We've been murderers ...': ibid., p. 340.

p. 49   'shame on the ...': ibid. p. 257.

p. 49   'when / Will such ...': Edmund Blunden, 'The Watchers', *Undertones of War*, p. 280.

p. 50   'For either side ...': *The Letters of Charles Hamilton Sorley* (Cambridge University Press, Cambridge, 1919), p. 283.

p. 50   'no shot was ...': quoted in Alan Clark, *The Donkeys*, p. 173.

p. 50   'a Saxon boy ...': *Wet Flanders Plain* p. 18.

p. 50   'German civilians sang ...': Arthur Bryant, *English Saga 1840–1940* (Collins, 1940), p. 292.

p. 51   'men whom the ...': Marc Ferro, *The Great War*, p. 225.

p. 51   'That was a ...': Friedrich Wilhelm Heinz, quoted in Eric J. Leed, *No Man's Land: Combat and Identity in World War 1*, p. 213.

p. 51   'The Dead are ...': Bob Bushaway, 'Name upon Name: The Great War and Remembrance, in Roy Porter (ed.), *Myths of the English*, p. 155.

p. 51   'disembodied rage ...', et al.: 'Beware the Unhappy Dead', *The Complete Poems* (Penguin, Harmondsworth, 1977), pp. 722–3.

p. 52   'The Third Reich ...': quoted in Marc Ferro, *The Great War*, p. 157.

p. 52   'the war changed ...': Samuel Gissing, quoted in Ronald Blythe, *Akenfield* (Penguin, Harmondsworth, 1972), p. 56.

p. 53   'They are all ...': letter to Catherine Carswell, 9 July 1916, *Selected Letters* (Penguin, Harmondsworth, 1950), p. 104.

p. 53   For further information on Private Ingham and other men executed, see Julian Putkowski and Julian Sykes, *Shot at Dawn*, pp. 138–40 *et passim*. See also Anthony Babington, *For the Sake of Example*.

p. 54   'My father was ...': Professor Jane Carter, 9 March 1993.

p. 55   For meticulous analysis of the faked sequences in *The Battle of the Somme* and other films see Roger Smither, ' "A wonderful idea of the fighting" ', *Imperial War Museum Review* no. 3, 1988, pp. 4–16.

p. 55   'every American character ...': *Hollywood's Vietnam* 2nd edn (Heinemann, 1989), p. 153.

p. 56   'masses of men ...': *A War Imagined: The First World War and English Culture*, p. 125.

p. 57   They are dead and they are going to die: I have adapted Roland Barthes' caption for Alexander Gardner's 1865 'Portrait of Lewis Payne', *Camera Lucida* (Hill & Wang, New York, 1981), p. 95.

p. 58   'I visualized an ...': *The Complete Memoirs of George Sherston*, p. 540.

p. 58   'The past is ...': *Requiem for a Nun* (Penguin, Harmondsworth, 1960), p. 81.

p. 58   'seemed more or ...': quoted in Denis Winter, *Death's Men*, p. 176.

p. 58   'the men appeared ...': ibid., p. 187.

p. 58   'like a sleepwalker ...': ibid. p. 189.

p. 58   'they come as ...': *In Parenthesis*, p. 170.

p. 58   'with strange eyes ...' and 'a rippling murmur ...': p. 210.

p. 58n 'fog-walkers ...': ibid., p. 179.

p. 59   'Now there came ...', et al.: *The Complete Memoirs of George Sherston*, p. 362.

p. 60   'mysterious army of . . .': *Akenfield* (Penguin, Harmondsworth, 1972), p. 33.

p. 60   'men clawed at . . .': quoted in Leon Wolff, *In Flanders Fields*, p. 124.

p. 60   'We marched and . . .': Ivor Gurney, 'Canadians', *Collected Poems*, p. 87.

p. 61   'Men became reminiscent . . .': quoted in Ann Compton (ed.), *Charles Sargeant Jagger: War and Peace Sculpture*, p. 78.

p. 64   'I heal . . .': ibid., p. 15.

p. 65   'Survivor outrage . . .' and 'Many survivors believe . . .': *The Texture of Memory: Holocaust Memorials and Meaning*, p. 9.

p. 66   'a sculptural language . . .': John Berger, *Art and Revolution* (Writers & Readers, 1969), p. 137. For an extended discussion of Zadkine's *Monument to Rotterdam* see Berger's *Permanent Red*, new edn (Writers & Readers, 1979), pp. 116–121.

p. 67n   'the sculptor who . . .', et al.: 'The Shape of Labour', *Art Monthly*, November 1986, pp. 4–8.

p. 68   'No man in . . .': General Harper, quoted in Denis Winter (who goes on to suggest that Harper was exaggerating), *Death's Men*, p. 110.

p. 69   'Leaning on his . . .': 'Lullaby of Cape Cod', *A Part of Speech* (Oxford University Press, Oxford, 1980), p. 109.

p. 69   'The angel does . . .': *And our Faces, My Heart, Brief as Photos* (Granta Books, 1992), p. 19.

p. 73   'to feel that . . .': F. Le Gros Clark, quoted in Samuel Hynes, *The Auden Generation*, p. 40.

p. 73   'terrific power . . .' and 'last word in . . .': quoted in Ann Compton (ed.), *Charles Sargeant Jagger: War and Peace Sculpture*, pp. 84–5.

p. 74   'it looked as . . .' and 'honourable scars of . . .': quoted in Peyton Skipwith, 'Gilbert Ledward R. A. and the Guards' Division Memorial', *Apollo*, January 1988, p. 26.

p. 76   ' . . . a khaki-clad leg . . .': p. 272.

p. 77   'after leaving him . . .': letter of 22 August 1917, *Collected Letters* p. 485.

p. 77   For Owen's use of Barbusse's images see Jon Stallworthy, *Wilfred Owen*, pp. 242–3 and p. 256.

p. 77   'I too saw ...': 'Apologia Pro Poemate Meo', *Collected Poems*, p. 39.

p. 77   'GAS! Quick, boys! ...': 'Dulce et Decorum Est', ibid., p. 55.

p. 77   'Mental Cases': ibid., p. 69.

p. 77   'S. I. W': ibid., p. 74.

p. 77   'Disabled': ibid., p. 67.

p. 77   'Red lips are ...': 'Greater Love', ibid., p. 41.

p. 77   'Futility': ibid., p. 58.

p. 78   'stuttering rifles' rapid ...': 'Anthem for Doomed Youth', ibid., p. 44.

p. 78   'spandau's manic jabber ...' and 'Straggling the road ...': *New and Collected Poems* (Robson Books, 1980), pp. 81–3.

p. 78   'Referring great success ...': quoted by Christopher Ridgway in introduction to Richard Aldington, *Death of a Hero*.

p. 79   'a pastiche of ...': quoted in Alex Dancher, ' "Bunking" and De-bunking', in Brian Bond (ed.), *The First World War and British Military History*, p. 49.

p. 79   'an imaginative leap ...' and 'live in the ...': *Strange Meeting*, p. 183.

p. 79   'Well there, I ...': ibid., p. 134.

p. 80   'I was always ...': pp. 143–4.

p. 80   'often hold their ...': Susan Hill, ibid., p. 149.

p. 80   'seemed unable to ...': *Birdsong*, p. 204.

p. 80   'Those fat pigs ...': ibid., p. 235.

p. 81   'ever-present dreamlike ...': *The Bells of Hell Go Ting-a-ling-a-ling*, p. 49.

p. 81   'Terrified, I clawed ...': ibid., p. 71.

p. 81   'not as factually ...':, p. 145.

p. 81   'if that wasn't ...': *The Bells of Hell Go Ting-a-ling-a-ling*, p. 49.

p. 82   'ears popped and ...': *The Wars*, p. 122.

p. 82   'What you people ...': ibid., pp. 46–7.

p. 83   'The mud. There ...': ibid., pp. 71–2.

p. 83   'a small train ...': *Birdsong*, p. 67.

p. 83   'from Albert out ...': ibid., p. 68.

p. 83   'where the Marne ...': ibid., p. 83.

p. 84   'terrible piling up ...': ibid., p. 59.

p. 84   The distinction between remembering and remembering the act of remembering together is derived from James E. Young, *The Texture of Memory*, p. 7.

p. 85   'the War itself . . .': *Lions and Shadows*, p. 296.

p. 85   'clean and new . . .': *Wet Flanders Plain*, p. 58.

p. 86   'Well might the . . .', et al.: 'On Passing the New Menin Gate', *Collected Poems*, p. 188.

p. 86   'sullen swamp . . .', et al.: p. 141 (my italics).

p. 87   'acute, shattering, the . . .': Armistice Day Supplement, 12 November 1920, p. i.

p. 87   'soul-shattering, heart-rending . . .': *Death of a Hero*, p. 34.

p. 87   'a terrible place . . .', et al.: *The Challenge of the Dead*, pp. 36–7.

p. 89   'memorial to all . . .' and 'mourns for all . . .': *Wet Flanders Plain*, pp. 97–8.

p. 90   'Now the chlorinated . . .' and 'the violent cough . . .': p. 130.

p. 91   'They sat or . . .': caption display next to Sargent's painting in the Imperial War Museum.

p. 91   'gargling from the . . .': 'Dulce et Decorum Est', *Collected Poems*, p. 55.

p. 91   For more on football, see Modris Eksteins, *Rites of Spring*, pp. 125–6.

p. 92   'There were many . . .': p. 144.

p. 92   'murmuring the name . . .': *Friends Apart*, p. 91 (italics in original).

p. 93   'litany of proper . . .': *The Tiger and the Rose* (Hamish Hamilton, 1971), p. 72.

p. 93   'Passchendaele, Bapaume, and . . .': 'The Great War', *New and Collected Poems* (Robson Books, 1980), p. 63.

p. 93   'Cambrai, Bethune, Arras . . .' and 'Passchendaele, Verdun, The . . .': 'The Guns', ibid., p. 110.

p. 93   'all things said . . .': 'Crucifix Corner', *Collected Poems*, p. 80; the other comparison, with Crickley, is in 'Poem for End', p. 201.

p. 93   'the copse was . . .': 'Near Vermand', ibid., p. 132.

p. 93   'Cotswold her spinnies . . .': from a different poem, also entitled 'Near Vermand', in Michael Hurd, *The Ordeal of Ivor Gurney*, p. 96.

p. 93   'a shattered wood ...': from a letter of June 1916, quoted in
        ibid., p. 72.

p. 93   'bad St Julien ...' et al.: *Collected Poems*, p. 170.

p. 94   'Tuesday, 2 October ...': *They Called It Passchendaele*, p. 189.

p. 94   'the names were ...': ibid., p. 187.

p. 94   '*The Oxford Book* ...': *Thank God for the Atom Bomb and Other
        Essays*, p. 101.

p. 94   'want of imagination ...': *The Great War and Modern Memory*,
        p. 12.

p. 94   'hopeless absence of ...' and 'entirely characteristic of ...':
        ibid., p. 13 (my italics).

p. 94   'it is refreshing ...': ibid., p. 109.

p. 95   'a sort of ...': ibid., p. 14.

p. 95   'the military equivalent ...': ibid., p. 12.

p. 95   'sophisticated observer ...': ibid., p. 6.

p. 95   ' "What 'appened to ...': *The Middle Parts of Fortune*, p. 219.

p. 96   'It was Christmas ...': *Oh What a Lovely War* (Methuen, 1965),
        p. 50.

p. 96   'They're warning us ...': ibid., p. 64.

p. 96   'those poor wounded ...' and 'sounds like a ...': ibid., pp. 88–9.

p. 96   'SECOND SOLDIER: What's ...': ibid., p.46.

p. 97   'And when they ...': ibid., p. 107.

p. 97   'it is really ...': *The Great War and Modern Memory*, p. 241.

p. 97   'the symbolism of ...': *The Complete Memoirs of George Sherston*,
        p. 325.

p. 98   'Aye, all's reet ...': quoted in *They Called It Passchendaele*, p. 201.

p. 98   'The salient was ...' and 'just a complete ...': ibid., p. 186.

p. 98   'To our dismay ...': *Wet Flanders Plain*, p. 99.

p. 99   'the flesh of ...': *Watermark* (Hamish Hamilton, 1992), p. 56;
        see also his poem 'Nature Morte', *A Part of Speech* (Oxford
        University Press, Oxford, 1980), p. 45.

p. 101 'concentrated essence of ...': Major-General J. F. C. Fuller,
        quoted in John Keegan, *The Face of Battle*, p. 232.

p. 103 'a merciless sea ...', et al.: *Short Stories*, vol. 2, edited by Andrew
        Rutherford (Penguin, Harmondsworth, 1971), p. 213.

p. 103 'Madame, please, / You ...': Brian Gardner (ed.), *Up the Line
        to Death*, p. 157.

p. 104 'the booming mecca ...': *They Called It Passchendaele*, p. 3.

p. 104 'earth gobs and ...', et al.: F. Scott Fitzgerald, *Tender is the Night*, pp. 125–6.

p. 104 'half–ironic phrase ...': ibid., p. 199.

p. 104 'A refuge for ...': ibid., p. 25.

p. 104 'the war is ...': ibid., p. 30.

p. 104 'was like all ...': ibid., p. 40.

p. 104 'I do not ...': letter to Henry Dan Piper, quoted in Matthew J. Bruccoli, *Some Kind of Epic Grandeur: The Life of F. Scott Fitzgerald*, revised edn (Cardinal, 1991), p. xix.

p. 104 'After all, life ...': letter to Mrs Richard Taylor, 10 June 1917, Andrew Turnbull (ed.), *The Letters of F. Scott Fitzgerald* (Penguin, 1968), p. 434.

p. 105 'shell–shocks who ...': *Tender is the Night*, p. 23.

p. 105 'a skull recently ...': ibid., p. 50.

p. 105 'Suddenly there was ...': ibid., p. 61.

p. 105 'Dick turned the ...' and 'See that little ...': ibid., pp. 124–5.

p. 107n For more on the Michael Foot/Cenotaph controversy see Patrick Wright's essay 'A Blue Plaque for the Labour Movement?', in *On Living in an Old Country*, Verso, 1985.

p. 110 'when events are ...': *The Texture of Memory*, p. 263.

p. 111 'The thousands of ...': Philip Larkin, 'MCMXIV', *Collected Poems* (Faber, 1988), p. 128.

p. 113 'the great everlasting ...': quoted in Modris Eksteins, *Rites of Spring*, p. 133.

p. 114 'had no pity ...': from introduction in Wilfred Owen, *Collected Poems*, pp. 18–19.

p. 114 ' "I've lost my ...': quoted in Denis Winter, *Death's Men*, p. 257.

p. 115 'The charred skeletons ...': Henri Barbusse, *War Diary*, in Jon Glover and Jon Silkin (eds.), *The Penguin Book of First World War Prose*, p. 197.

p. 115 'the most extraordinary ...': letter of 13 May 1916, *Winds of Change* (Macmillan, 1966), p. 82.

p. 115 'shells never seem ...': Julian Symons (ed.), *The Essential Wyndham Lewis*, p. 23.

p. 115 'the famous Cloth ...': Gunner B. O. Stokes, quoted in Lyn Macdonald, *They Called It Passchendaele*, p. 190.

p. 115 'One ever hangs ...': 'At a Calvary near the Ancre', Wilfred Owen, *Collected Poems*, p. 82.

p. 115 'The Calvary stood ...': Jon Glover and Jon Silkin (eds.), *The Penguin Book of First World War Prose*, p. 145.

p. 116 'The cemetery at ...': quoted in Michael Hurd, *The Ordeal of Ivor Gurney* p. 69.

p. 116 'like the edge ...' and 'the trees of ...': *The Complete Memoirs of George Sherston*, p. 279.

p. 117 'a landscape of ...': quoted in Robert Rosenblum, *Modern Painting and the Northern Romantic Tradition* (Thames & Hudson, 1978), p. 29.

p. 117 Robert Musil: diary entry for 3 September 1915, *Tagebucher*, (Rowohlt Verlag, Reinbeck bei Hamburg, 1976), p. 312; translation in Jon Glover and Jon Silkin (eds.), *The Penguin Book of First World War Prose*, p. 95.

p. 117 'a sea of ...': Lieutenant J. W. Naylor, quoted in Lyn Macdonald, *They Called It Passchendaele*, p. 188.

p. 117 'a dead sea ...': *Undertones of War*, p. 221.

p. 118 'land-ocean': *The Challenge of the Dead*, p. 24.

p. 118 'As you look ...': quoted in Kevin Brownlow, *The War, the West and the Wilderness*, p. 148.

p. 118 'By any earlier ...': *Modern Painting and the Northern Romantic Tradition* (Thames & Hudson, 1978), p. 13.

p. 120 'skinned, gouged, flayed ...': Peter Vansittart (ed.), *Letters from the Front* (Constable, 1984), p. 217.

p. 120 'In point of ...': p. 150.

p. 120 'plain of lost ...': *War Diary*, in Jon Glover and Jon Silkin (eds.), *The Penguin Book of First World War Prose*, p. 150.

p. 120 'The old church ...': *The Challenge of the Dead*, p. 256.

p. 120 'In a later ...': *In Flanders Fields*, p. 296.

p. 120 'Aerial photos of ...': *Haig's Command*, p. 46.

p. 121 The vanished villages of Verdun: for an evocation of the topographical and historical legacy of Verdun see the last two parts – 'Aftermath' and 'Epilogue' – of Alistair Horne, *The Price of Glory: Verdun 1916*.

p. 121 'Theory of Ruin ...': *Inside the Third Reich* (Sphere, 1971), pp. 97–8.

p. 121   'special teams spent . . .': *The Rebel* (Penguin, Harmondsworth, 1971), p. 154.

p. 122   'a sponge, an . . .': Jean Rouaud, *Fields of Glory*, p. 133.

p. 122   'I am beginning . . .': diary entry for 7 October, quoted in Trevor Wilson, *The Myriad Faces of War*, p. 751.

p. 122   'We didn't really . . .': John Grout, quoted in Ronald Blythe, *Akenfield* (Penguin, Harmondsworth, 1972), p. 62.

p. 122   'reveals hardly the . . .': Denis Winter, *Death's Men*, p. 255.

p. 122   'what the Nazis . . .', et al.: 'Messages in a Bottle', *New Left Review* (no. 200, July/August 1993), p. 6.

p. 124   'trees not quite . . .': p. 18.

p. 124   'when the trenches . . .': *The Old Frontline* (Heinemann, 1917), p. 11.

p. 124   'all semblance gone . . .': *Journey to the Western Front, Twenty Years After* (G. Bell & Son, 1936), p. 1.

p. 124   'Nature herself conspires . . .': Paul Berry and Alan Bishop (eds.), *Testament of a Generation: The Journalism of Vera Brittain and Winifred Holtby* (Virago, 1985), p. 210.

p. 124   'And pile them . . .': Archibald MacLeish (ed.), *The Complete Poems* (Harcourt Brace Jovanovich, New York, 1970), p. 136.

p. 125   'A farmer on . . .': *The English Patient* (Bloomsbury, 1992), p. 123.

p. 125   'the ground breaks . . .': 'A Calvary on the Somme', *Selected Poems* (Bloodaxe, Newcastle, 1991), p. 135.

p. 126   'Corpses, rats, old . . .': Peter Vansittart (ed.), *Letters from the Front* (Constable, 1984), p. 263.

p. 127   'From that moment . . .': quoted in Martin Middlebrook, *The First Day on the Somme*, p. 316.

p. 127   'These apparently rude . . .': *The Middle Parts of Fortune*, p. 205.

p. 128   'The century of . . .': a revised version of this lecture was published as 'Ev'ry Time we Say Goodbye' in *Keeping a Rendez-vous*, Granta 1992.

p. 130   'there are more . . .': *The Plague* (Penguin, Harmondsworth, 1948), p. 251.

SELECT BIBLIOGRAPHY

Books quoted in the text with no real connection with the war or the main themes of the book are not listed here; nor are volumes of poetry which happen to contain the odd poem about the war. Bibliographical details for these titles are given in the Notes. Place of publication is London unless stated otherwise.

FICTION, MEMOIRS, POETRY

Aldington, Richard, *Death of a Hero*, Hogarth, 1984.

Barbusse, Henri, *Under Fire*, trans. W. Fitzwater Wray, Dent, 1988.

Barker, Pat, *Regeneration*, Viking, 1991.

Barker, Pat, *The Eye in the Door*, Viking, 1993.

Blunden, Edmund, *Undertones of War*, Penguin, Harmondsworth, 1982.

Chapman, Guy, *A Passionate Prodigality*, Buchan & Enright, Southampton, 1985.

Faulks, Sebastian, *Birdsong*, Hutchinson, 1993.

Findley, Timothy, *The Wars*, Penguin, Harmondsworth, 1978.

Fitzgerald, F. Scott, *Tender is the Night*, Penguin, Harmondsworth, 1955.

Graham, Stephen, *The Challenge of the Dead*, Cassell, 1921.

Graves, Robert, *Goodbye to All That*, Penguin, Harmondsworth, 1960.

Gurney, Ivor, *Collected Poems*, ed. P. J. Kavanagh, Oxford University Press, Oxford, 1982.

Gurney, Ivor, *War Letters*, ed. R. K. R. Thornton, Hogarth, 1984.

Hemingway, Ernest, *A Farewell to Arms*, Penguin, Harmondsworth, 1935.

Hill, Susan, *Strange Meeting*, Penguin, Harmondsworth, 1989.

Hiscock, Eric, *The Bells of Hell Go Ting-a-ling-a-ling*, Arlington Books, 1976.

Isherwood, Christopher, *Lions and Shadows*, Hogarth, 1938.

Jones, David, *In Parenthesis*, Faber, 1987.

Manning, Frederic, *The Middle Parts of Fortune* (also known as *Her Privates We*), Buchan & Enright, Southampton, 1986.

Owen, Wilfred, *Collected Poems*, edited with an introduction and notes by C. Day Lewis and a Memoir by Edmund Blunden, Chatto & Windus, 1963.

Owen, Wilfred, *Collected Letters*, edited by Harold Owen and John Bell, Oxford University Press, Oxford, 1967.

Owen, Wilfred, *The Complete Poems and Fragments*, 2 vols., edited by Jon Stallworthy, Oxford University Press, Oxford, 1983.

Remarque, Erich Maria, *All Quiet on the Western Front*, trans. A. W. Wheen, Picador, 1987.

Rosenberg, Isaac, *Collected Works*, Chatto & Windus, 1984.

Rouaud, Jean, *Fields of Glory*, trans. Ralph Manheim, Collins Harvill, 1992.

Sassoon, Siegfried, *Siegfried's Journey 1916–1920*, Faber, 1945.

Sassoon, Siegfried, *Collected Poems 1908–1956*, Faber, 1961.

Sassoon, Siegfried, *The Complete Memoirs of George Sherston*, Faber, 1972.

Sassoon, Siegfried, *Diaries 1915–1918*, ed. Rupert Hart-Davis, Faber, 1983.

Toynbee, Philip, *Friends Apart*, MacGibbon & Kee, 1954.

HISTORIES AND CULTURAL STUDIES

Anderson, Benedict, *Imagined Communities*, Verso, 1983.

Babington, Anthony, *For the Sake of Example*, Leo Cooper/Secker & Warburg, 1983.

Bergonzi, Bernard, *Heroes' Twilight*, Constable, 1965.

Bond, Brian (ed.), *The First World War and British Military History*, Oxford University Press, Oxford, 1991.

Boorman, Derek, *At the Going Down of the Sun: British First World War Memorials*, Sessions, York, 1988.

Borg, Alan, *War Memorials*, Leo Cooper, 1991.

Brownlow, Kevin, *The War, the West and the Wilderness*, Secker & Warburg, 1979.

Bushaway, Bob, 'Name upon Name: The Great War and Remembrance', in Roy Porter (ed.), *Myths of the English*, Polity, Cambridge, 1992.

Cannadine, David, 'Death, Grief and Mourning in Modern Britain', in Joachim Whalley (ed.), *Mirrors of Mortality*, Europa, 1984.

Capa, Robert, *Photographs*, edited by Richard Whelan and Cornell Capa, Faber, 1985.

Carmichael, Jane, *First World War Photographers*, Routledge, 1989.

Clark, Alan, *The Donkeys*, Pimlico, 1991.

Compton, Ann (ed.), *Charles Sargeant Jagger: War and Peace Sculpture*, Imperial War Museum, 1985.

Coombs, Rose E. B., *Before Endeavours Fade*, After the Battle Publications, 1976.

Eksteins, Modris, *Rites of Spring*, Bantam, 1989.

Elsen, Albert E., *Modern European Sculpture 1918–1945: Unknown Beings and Other Realities*, Braziller, New York, 1979.

Ferro, Marc, *The Great War*, Routledge, 1973.

Foot, M. R. D., *Art and War*, Headline, 1990.

Fussell, Paul, *The Great War and Modern Memory*, Oxford University Press, Oxford, 1975.

Fussell, Paul, *Thank God for the Atom Bomb and Other Essays*, Ballantine, New York, 1990.

Garrett, Richard, *The Final Betrayal*, Buchan & Enright, Southampton, 1989.

Harries, Meirion and Susie, *War Artists*, Michael Joseph, 1983.

Hibberd, Dominic, *Wilfred Owen: The Last Year*, Constable, 1992.

Horne, Alistair, *The Price of Glory: Verdun 1916*, Penguin, Harmondsworth, 1964.

Hurd, Michael, *The Ordeal of Ivor Gurney*, Oxford University Press, Oxford, 1978.

Hynes, Samuel, *A War Imagined: The First World War and English Culture*, Bodley Head, 1990.

Hynes, Samuel, *The Auden Generation*, Pimlico, 1992.

Keegan, John, *The Face of Battle*, Cape, 1976.

Kern, Stephen, *The Culture of Time and Space 1880–1918*, Harvard University Press, Cambridge, 1983.

Larkin, Philip, *Required Writing*, Faber, 1983.

Leed, Eric J., *No Man's Land: Combat and Identity in World War 1*, Cambridge University Press, Cambridge, 1979.

Liddell Hart, B. H., *History of the First World War*, Cassell, 1970.

Longworth, Philip, *The Unending Vigil*, Constable, 1967.

Macdonald, Lyn, *They Called It Passchendaele*, Michael Joseph, 1978.

Macdonald, Lyn, *The Roses of No Man's Land*, Michael Joseph, 1980.

Macdonald, Lyn, *Somme*, Michael Joseph, 1983.

Macdonald, Lyn, *1914*, Michael Joseph, 1987.

Middlebrook, Martin, *The First Day on the Somme*, Penguin, Harmondsworth, 1984.

Middlebrook, Martin and Mary, *The Somme Battlefields*, Viking, 1991.

Moeller, Susan, *Shooting War*, Basic Books, New York, 1990.

Mosse, George, *Fallen Soldiers: Reshaping the Memory of the World Wars*, Oxford University Press, Oxford, 1990.

Orwell, George, *The Collected Essays, Journalism and Letters*, Volume 1, Penguin, Harmondsworth, 1970.

Parker, Peter, *The Old Lie: The Great War and the Public School Ethos*, Constable, 1987.

Pick, Daniel, *War Machine: The Rationalisation of Slaughter in the Modern Age*, Yale University Press, New Haven, 1993.

Putkowski, Julian, and Sykes, Julian, *Shot at Dawn*, revised edn, Leo Cooper, 1992.

Robbins, Keith, *The First World War*, Oxford University Press, Oxford, 1984.

Scarry, Elaine, *The Body in Pain*, Oxford University Press, Oxford, 1985.

Silkin, Jon, *Out of Battle*, 2nd edn, Ark, 1987.

Stallworthy, Jon, *Wilfred Owen*, Oxford University Press, Oxford, 1974.

Symons, Julian (ed.), *The Essential Wyndham Lewis*, André Deutsch, 1989.

Taylor, A. J. P., *The First World War*, Penguin, Harmondsworth, 1966.

Terraine, John, *The First World War 1914–18*, Macmillan, 1984.

Viney, Nigel, *Images of Wartime*, David & Charles, Newton Abbot, 1991.

Virilio, Paul, *War and Cinema*, trans. Patrick Camiller, Verso, 1989.

Warner, Philip, *Field Marshal Earl Haig*, Bodley Head, 1991.

Whelan, Richard, *Robert Capa: A Biography*, Faber, 1985.

Williamson, Henry, *Wet Flanders Plain*, Gliddon, Norwich, 1989.

Wilson, Trevor, *The Myriad Faces of War*, Polity, Cambridge, 1986.

Winter, Denis, *Death's Men*, Penguin, Harmondsworth, 1979.

Winter, Denis, *Haig's Command*, Viking, 1991.

Wolff, Leon, *In Flanders Fields*, Penguin, Harmondsworth, 1979.

Young, James E., *The Texture of Memory: Holocaust Memorials and Meaning*, Yale University Press, New Haven, 1993.

Fussell, Paul, *The Bloody Game*, Scribners, 1991.

Gardner, Brian, *Up the Line to Death*, revised edn, Methuen, 1976.

Glover, Jon, and Silkin, Jon, *The Penguin Book of First World War Prose*, Penguin, Harmondsworth, 1989.

Macdonald, Lyn, *1914–1918: Voices and Images from the Great War*, Michael Joseph, 1988.

Silkin, Jon, *The Penguin Book of First World War Poetry*, 2nd edn, Penguin, Harmondsworth, 1981.

Stallworthy, Jon, *The Oxford Book of War Poetry*, Oxford University Press, Oxford, 1988.

Vansittart, Peter, *Voices from the Great War*, Cape, 1981.

INDEX